ARNOT ART MUSEUM
Elmira, New York

1989

A Collector's

Vision

THE 1910 BEQUEST OF MATTHIAS H. ARNOT

Rachael Sadinsky

ARNOT ART MUSEUM
BOARD OF TRUSTEES

Sidney J. Mann, Ph.D., *President*
Thomas D. Morse, *Vice President*
Lewis W. Morse, Jr., *Vice President*
Mrs. Alexander D. Falck, Jr., *Secretary*
Jan P. Updegraff, *Treasurer*
William C. Beck, M.D.
Mrs. Edward V. Bennett
Alexander D. Falck, III
Mrs. Darwin C. Farber
Thomas W. Gardner
Herbert W. Gledhill
Robert L. Ivers
Kevin Kennedy
Stuart Komer
Thomas Meier, Ph.D.
Mrs. Joseph S. Pierce
Elbert W. Ryerson
Allen C. Smith
Mrs. Gillett Welles
Mrs. Murray J. Werner
Mrs. Jeffrey Yunis

HONORARY TRUSTEES

J. Rathbone Falck
Howard H. Kimball, Jr.
Mrs. S. Roberts Rose

© 1989 Arnot Art Museum. All rights reserved. No part of this publication may be reproduced in any manner whatsoever without permission in writing by the Arnot Art Museum.

Library of Congress Cataloguing-in-Publication Data

Sadinsky, Rachael, 1958-
    A collector's vision : the 1910 bequest of Matthias H. Arnot / Rachael Sadinsky.
        p.   cm.
      Bibliography: p.
      Includes index.
      1. Painting, European—Catalogs. 2. Painting, Modern—Europe—Catalogs. 3. Arnot, Matthias Hollenback, 1833-1910—Art collections--Catalogs. 4. Painting—Private collections—New York (State)—Elmira—Catalogs. 5. Arnot Art Museum—Catalogs. I. Arnot, Matthias Hollenback, 1833-1910. II. Arnot Art Museum. III. Title.
    ND160.S23 1989
    759.94′074′74778—dc20   89-15178
                                                  CIP

ISBN 1-877885-05-3

Cover: Matthias Hollenback Arnot with marble bust of John Arnot, Sr. in picture gallery, ca. 1900.
Frontispiece: The Arnot residence, Elmira, ca. 1900.

JEAN-LEON GEROME, The Marabou (At the Door of His House)

EMILIO SANCHEZ-PERRIER, By the River (Alcala)

FOREWORD

The Arnot Art Museum is one of a very few museums in this country that has made it a policy to maintain intact the original collection of its founder. That founder, Matthias H. Arnot, was not unlike other collectors in the late nineteenth century. A successful businessman, he enjoyed collecting works of art and living with them in his home. Over the first 75 years of the Museum's history, there have been several versions of a collection catalogue. The Trustees believe that a significant portion of our mission is to provide a base of information for the consideration of the collector, his motivation as well as his life and times. Earlier versions of the collection catalogue have not delved into the persona of this individual nor have they presented the founding collection so completely.

The Museum has a commitment to conducting research relative to its collection and to updating collection publications. The catalogue of an institution's collection, whether it be paintings or automobiles, should present to the reader an image of that institution at a given moment in time. This image should be multidimensional in order to provide the reader with a more complete impression than would have been gained through a visit. Such is the case with this volume. Matthias Arnot is portrayed as an individual interested in collecting and sharing his collection with the public; his founding collection is presented herein along with the provenance for each piece.

For historians, researchers, and those interested in the arts in general, this volume is invaluable. For the people of Elmira, it provides a detailed view of their cultural heritage.

Sidney J. Mann
President of the Board of Trustees

JULES-ADOLPHE BRETON, Le Soir

ACKNOWLEDGEMENTS

This project would not have been possible without the support and encouragement of the latter-day Arnot family. I am especially grateful to Mrs. Natalie Falck for generously supplying source material on the Arnot family and for correcting factual errors in the introductory text. I am also indebted to John Brand II, John Brand III, Mary Brand Kemberling, and Nancy Brand Barringer whose contributions to the Harriet Hoffman Brand Fund aided in providing the resources necessary for the completion of this project. The Board of Trustees and the staff of the Arnot Art Museum have been very supportive. Dr. Sidney Mann and Dr. William C. Beck read the text and offered valuable insight. Shelley Wead, Administrative Assistant, was essential in readying the text for publication. Tom Janowski, Registrar, and Mike Carpenter facilitated the hectic demands of photographing and installing the collection. This catalogue benefited from the contributions of other scholars and researchers. In the introductory text, I am grateful for the advice and source documents provided by Susan Brady, Yale University; Ann K. Sindelar, Western Reserve Historical Society; Georgia Gy. Toth, Cleveland Museum of Art; Henry J. Duffy, Marymount College; and Michael Helston, National Gallery, London. Several scholars offered their suggestions on the various interpretations of individual artists and they are cited in the appropriate catalogue entries. Special thanks go to Cara Sutherland, Chemung County Historical Society, for her willingness to share her knowledge of Victorian Elmira and for graciously agreeing to read and comment upon the text. I am also thankful for the creative talents of Lesli Van Zandbergen in photographing the Arnot collection. In the publication of the catalogue, Jill Elyse Grossvogel has, as in the past, given me the benefit of her expertise and careful attention to detail.

Rachael Sadinsky
Curator of Collections

CLAUDE LORRAIN, Ariadne and Bacchus on Naxos (Ulysses Discovering Himself to Nausicaa)

JEAN-BAPTISTE DE CHAMPAIGNE, The Stoning of St. Paul

JAN BRUEGHEL, THE ELDER, A Flemish Fair

JAN BRUEGHEL, THE ELDER and JOHANN ROTTENHAMMER, Venus and Apollo, Putti Dancing

DAVID TENIERS, THE YOUNGER, Interior of a Kitchen

WILLEM VAN DE VELDE, THE YOUNGER, Man-of-War in a Storm

ANTHONIE DE LORME, Interior of a Church

JEAN-FRANCOIS MILLET, Apple Gatherers

GUSTAVE COURBET, A Mountain Stream

CHARLES-FRANCOIS DAUBIGNY, On the Oise

NARCISSE VIRGILE DIAZ DE LA PENA, In the Pyrenées

JEAN-LOUIS-ERNEST MEISSONIER, The Stirrup Cup

JEAN-LOUIS-ERNEST MEISSONIER, Playing Bowles in the Fosse at Antibes

JEHAN-GEORGES VIBERT, The Cardinal's Menu

JEAN-JOSEPH BENJAMIN-CONSTANT, Messaline

JULES-EMILE SAINTIN, Two Oracles

LUDWIG KNAUS, The Child's Funeral

INTRODUCTION

I direct my executors

hereinafter named and appointed . . .

to cause to be created

and organized under the

proper statute or statutes of the

State of New York,

a corporation with the name Arnot Art Gallery . . . .[1]

1 *Last Will and Testament*, April 2, 1908, p. 2.

2 *Memorandum for the Trustees of the Arnot Art Gallery*, dated posthumously by the executors of the estate of Matthias Arnot, April 29, 1910, p. 1.

With these words, Matthias Hollenback Arnot (1893-1910) initiated what was to become his most enduring act of public service for Elmira: he bequeathed the city and its inhabitants his art collection and home. During the last three decades of the nineteenth century, he assembled a collection of over seventy paintings, half a dozen sculptures, and a handful of Egyptian and Greek artifacts. Arnot acquired choice examples of Old Masters and contemporary Salon artists, similar to many other American collectors of this period. It is one of the few of these collections still together and housed in the setting for which it was originally intended. Arnot's collection grew primarily from the sales of other noteworthy private collections, suggesting he was as interested in acquiring the art as he was in assuming the cachet of a work's previous owner. After years of personal enjoyment, it was Matthias Arnot's wish to share his wealth with the residents of Elmira and surrounding regions rather than selling the collection or keeping it solely in family hands. His 1910 bequest instructed his executors and trustees of what was to become the Arnot Art Gallery to convert the ancestral Arnot home into a gallery with free access to the general public for "whatever enjoyment or mental or moral elevation such an institution may bestow."[2] The intention of such a generous and democratic act has its roots in the social context of late nineteenth-century America, reflecting Matthias Arnot's commitment to the obligations of wealth and the responsibilities of social class.

Matthias Hollenback Arnot was the youngest son in one of the more prominent and influential families of Elmira. His father, John Arnot, Sr. (1789/93-1873), was an enterprising Scottish immigrant who came to the area on a mercantile venture and went on to manufacturing, real estate, and banking (he was one of the founders and, later, the owner of the Chemung Canal Bank). As industrialization progressed, John Arnot, Sr. prospered. He invested heavily in the Erie and Northern Central railroads, as well as in the region's canals, roads, and utilities. By the time of his death in 1873, the village of Elmira had become a city and John Arnot had amassed a fortune reputedly worth over $15 million. The Arnot children, well-trained by their father for the duties of managing and increasing the family fortune, were also concerned with giving something back to the area and the people from whom they profited. The oldest child, Marianna Tuttle Arnot (1825-1904) founded the Elmira Industrial School in 1877 to provide vocational training for the poor. In 1888, she established the Arnot-Ogden Memorial Hospital to give a home to the Elmira Academy of Medicine, a group of doctors dedicated to providing medical care to Elmira's sick and indigent.[3] John Arnot's two eldest sons, Stephen Tuttle Arnot (1829-1884) and John Arnot, Jr., (1831-1886), devoted themselves to politics and public service. Stephen was a prominent alderman for the city for many years and became mayor in 1883, serving out the unexpired term of David B. Hill, who had been elected Lieutenant-Governor of the state. John Arnot, Jr. was elected president of the village in 1859 and later the first mayor of the city of Elmira in 1864, a post he held until 1878. In 1882 and again in 1884, he was elected to Congress, serving as Democratic Representative in the House.[4]

Matthias Arnot, unlike his brothers, did not care much for public life or publicity. He graduated from Yale in 1856 with a thorough grounding in the classics, history, and philosophy. After college, he returned to Elmira and went to work at the family bank. In time, he became president of the bank and assumed responsibility over all the family business concerns. He also performed his civic duty by serving on the board of area institutions including the local Board of Education, the New York State Reformatory, and, as might be expected, his sister's institution, the Arnot-Ogden Memorial Hospital. He never married and was devoted to his work. He did socialize with his peers, however, through memberships in several private clubs in Elmira and New York City, including the Union, Manhattan, and Metropolitan clubs.[5] He was known for his generous, albeit anonymous, acts of charity. His obituary in the *Fifty-Sixth Anniversary of the Class of Fifty-Six, Yale* describes several examples of Arnot's financial generosity, including:

... a loan to a worthy but unfortunate young man threatened with foreclosure and the loss of his business, of a generous sum to put him on his feet . . .
... his tenant of twenty years, who for the first time could not pay his rent, [and his] surprise on receiving a quit-claim deed of the house and farm he occupied . . . .[6]

The Elmira papers also described his generosity in "handsome bequests under the name of 'a friend' or 'cash'" but added that Arnot was a shrewd judge of character and "rarely ever failed to make correct estimate of a person."[7]

Arnot's taste in art and his desire to collect it are emblematic of his generation's impulses. At mid-century, it was fashionable to build collections of the contemporary arts of both America and Europe. After the Civil War, however, America's elite looked exclusively to Europe as America's limited artistic heritage only increased collectors' envy of the old world's cultural legacy.[8] Eager to show their own refinement and appreciation of high culture, Americans of means flocked to Europe and returned home with artworks as souvenirs of their Grand Tour. American collectors acquired art for a variety of reasons: enhancement of their prestige as connoisseurs; furnishing the picture galleries in their newly-built mansions with evidence of an aristocratic heritage; genuine appreciation of the art object and the desire to improve American culture by importing the best of Europe's art. What appealed to America's affluent were works of a guaranteed worth that promised both artistic and financial value. Paintings by Old Masters were always a safe choice and often the first significant acquisitions of collectors eager to buy quality. But the strongest impulse in late nineteenth-century America was to collect works by contemporary French and German artists whose popularity and professional successes in the Salon exhibitions assured their value.

The Salon, the annual (occasionally bi-annual) exhibition sponsored by the French government, was at the peak of its importance in the last half of the nineteenth century.[9] It was an enormous art extravaganza held in the Palais de l'Industrie and the focus of worldwide attention as tourists, art lovers, collectors, critics, and dealers came to Paris to see the new and the best in contemporary art. The Salon, so called because the early exhibitions were held in the Grand Salon of the Louvre, originated in 1699 as an exhibition of the artists in the Académie des Beaux-Arts, the fine arts section of the national academic establishment, the Institut de France. After the Revolution and during the course of the nineteenth century, the government introduced several reforms to make the Salon more democratic and available to all artists. In the era before art dealers and sales galleries, Salons were the only means by which artists could show their works to the public. Acceptance into the Salon was crucial for the advancement of one's career. Admission was competitive, the jury being comprised of public officials and artists. Further glory for exhibitors came in the form of prize medals, commissions, appointments to the Legion of Honor, and state purchases. Political maneuvering by ambitious jurors could alter the career of an artist as some championed their friends and students while forcing blanket rejections of a particular artist or school. For the most part, juries maintained academic standards and showed a marked preference for those artists who had undergone the rigorous training at the Ecole des Beaux-Arts. The Ecole had a formalized program of art instruction based on competitions and regimented study of the figure and composition, which culminated in the ultimate contest, the Prix de Rome, a three year scholarship to

3   The hospital was named in honor of Marianna Arnot's late husband, William Butler Ogden (1805-1877), one of the founders of Chicago and that city's first mayor.

4   John Arnot, Jr., was unable to serve out his second term in Congress due to an injury he suffered in a gas explosion at the Chemung Canal Bank. His marriage to Anne Elizabeth Hulett (1837-1901/07) produced four children and thereby provided for the continuance of the Arnot line through to the present day. One of their children, Matthias Charles Arnot (1867-1901) is often confused with Matthias Hollenback Arnot in local history books and newspaper accounts of the family. Like his uncle, Matthias Charles was a Yale graduate, however, it was Matthias Charles, not Matthias Hollenback, who was an enthusiastic supporter of aeronautics and funded the experiments of Professor A.M. Herring of St. Joseph, Missouri.
    Stephen Tuttle Arnot married Charlotte Hewitt (1828-1911) and their granddaughter, Charlotte Whitney Allen (1891-1978) founded the Charlotte Whitney Allen Library of the Memorial Art Gallery, University of Rochester.
    Very little is known of the two remaining Arnot children. Aurelia Covell Arnot (1827-1874) never married and most likely spent her life running her bachelor brother Matthias' home. Fanny Arnot (1834-1919) married George Griswold Haven (? -1908), a prominent New York City banker and president of the Metropolitan Opera and Real Estate Company.

5   The Metropolitan Club was founded by J.P. Morgan and, according to Betsy Brint, Secretary to the Metropolitan Club, "only acquaintances of Morgan were considered for membership." I am grateful to both Ms. Brint and Mrs. Helen Allen, Librarian for the Union Club, for information.

6   *Fifty-Sixth Anniversary of the Class of Fifty-Six, Yale* (New Haven: Yale University Press, 1912), p. 18.

7   *Elmira Telegram*, February 20, 1910.

8   For an introduction to Victorian art patronage, see Lillian B. Miller, *Patrons and Patriotism: The Encouragement of the Fine Arts in the United States* (Chicago: University of Chicago Press, 1966), Part IV: Patrons and Taste, and W.G. Constable, *Art Collecting in the United States of America: An Outline of History* (NY: Thomas Nelson and Sons, Ltd., 1964), Chapter VI: French Art.
    For a description of over ninety American collectors and their collections, see Edward Strahan [Earl Shinn], *The Art Treasures of America*, 3 vols. (Philadelphia: George Barrie, 1880). The three-volume publication had one thousand subscribers, including three from Elmira, J.S. Fassett, Alexander Diven, and H.W. Rathbone.

9   The history of the Académie des Beaux-Arts, the Ecole des Beaux-Arts, and the Salon exhibitions has been well-documented. Good recent accounts include: Albert Boime, *The Academy and French Painting in the Nineteenth Century* (New Haven: Yale University Press, 1986), Eric Zafran, *French Salon Paintings from Southern Collections*, introd. Gerald Ackerman (Atlanta: The High Museum of Art, 1982); and James Harding, *Artistes Pompiers: French Academic Art in the 19th Century* (London: Academy Editions, [1979]).

10 The editors of Samuel P. Avery's diaries provided an enormously helpful introductory essay which describes Avery's life and career as well as his impact on the American art buying public, including statistical analyses of Avery's sales by subject matter, price, and home and occupation of Avery's clients. *The Diaries, 1871-1882, of Samuel P. Avery, Art Dealer*, ed. and intro. Madeleine Fidell Beaufort, Herbert L. Kleinfield, and Jeanne K. Welcher (NY: Arno Press, 1979), pp. xxxv-xxxviii.

11 Avery, like Arnot, belonged to the Metropolitan and Manhattan clubs. *The Diaries, 1871-1882, of Samuel P. Avery, Art Dealer*, p. xxvi.

12 Samuel P. Avery, Jr. continued in the business of art dealing after his father retired in 1885 and Arnot's purchases most likely date from this period, the late 1880s or the 1890s.

13 During the last quarter of the nineteenth century, affluent Americans were more supportive of their native artists when they traveled abroad when they could visit artists' studios and purchase or commission works. See Neil Harris, *The Artist in American Society: The Formative Years, 1790-1860* (NY: George Braziller, Inc., 1966), pp. 284-298, and Meredith Ward, *Adventure and Inspiration: American Artists in Other Lands* (NY: Hirschl and Adler Galleries, Inc., 1988).

For a discussion of the appeal for C.B. Ives' portraits by wealthy tourists, see Lorado Taft, *The History of American Sculpture* (NY: MacMillan Co., 1903), pp. 112-113, and Wayne Craven, *Sculpture in America* (NY: Thomas and Crowell, 1968), pp. 284-288.

14 Arnot's purchases from the Centennial Exposition were not, however, of uniform quality as his acquisition of O.T. Cyphas (?), *The Chimney Sweep* (acc. no. 68) demonstrates.

For the Eggert and Meyer von Bremen references, see: *The Masterpieces of the Centennial International Exhibition*, vol. 1: *Fine Art* by Edward Strahan [Earl Shinn], vol. 2: *Industrial Art* by Walter Smith, vol. 3: *History, Mechanics, and Science* by Joseph Miller Wilson (Philadelphia: Gebbie and Barrie, 1876-1878; reprint ed., NY: Garland Publishing Co., 1977), 1: 208, illus. p. 153, and James D. McCabe, *The Illustrated History of the Centennial* (Philadelphia: The National Publishing Company, 1876), p. 593.

15 The May 27-June 21, 1879, exhibition was held in the Elmira Opera House. Admission was two shillings for a one-time entry while a season ticket was one dollar for women and two dollars for men. The *Elmira Daily Advertiser* (June 23, 1879) reported the event earned "in the neighborhood of two thousand dollars." The

study in Rome. The aim of the Ecole was to make artists proficient in specific techniques of painting (such as idealized forms, conservative colors, and highly finished surfaces) and fully versed in subjects considered to be intellectually ennobling. The Ecole is credited with giving technical facility to a great many artists often at the price of discouraging individual excellence by breeding conformity to one set of standards. During the course of the nineteenth century, the number of skilled artists grew and by mid-century the Salon was enormous: the Salon of 1880 exhibited over seven thousand works of which nearly four thousand were paintings.

Success at the Salon brought a secondary but no less attractive prize: patronage by an increasingly affluent public. Artists were quick to recognize that this market was able to afford the art which appealed to them but was often without the literary or artistic education of the academic masters and Salon jurors. History painting, long considered to be an artist's highest achievement and proof of both his skill and education, did not appeal to the bourgeois audience. The public favored works that spoke to the heart rather than the mind and styles that captured the appearance of reality without suggesting the harshness of the real world. The pressures of modernity—mechanization, labor troubles, political activism and revolutions—made traditional art with its beautiful, idealized figures and refined subjects increasingly popular. Sentimental paintings with an educational or emotional content, painted in a way that was easily understood by any and all viewers, commanded high prices. The most successful artists supplied the public with soothing, pleasant subjects or good stories that were morally elevating without causing discomfort or offending delicate sensibilities. Moreover, the patron was assured that he was receiving a well-crafted work as befitted an artist who had dedicated years of study to his profession. The flawless finish of a meticulously detailed painting illustrated the artist's grasp of anatomy and composition and his expertise in painterly techniques.

The Ecole and the Salon jurors continued to award its highest praise for history paintings but also acknowledged and awarded prizes to the best paintings of subjects catering to a more general audience. Genre paintings of everyday life were a broad-based and popular field encompassing the historical costume pieces of J.L.E. Meissonier, Vibert's gentle satires of religious genre, and the sentimental peasant genre scenes of Millet and Breton. German genre painters, such as Ludwig Knaus and Meyer von Bremen, were especially popular for their meticulous attention to detail, intimate scale, and accessible, anecdotal subjects. The wild and farm animal subjects of the *animalier* painters and sculptors, such as Rosa Bonheur and Barye, and the landscapes of the Barbizon artists found a receptive public on both sides of the Atlantic: the collectors nostalgic for scenes of a pre-industrial countryside. *Orientaliste* subjects of Moorish Spain, Greece, and the Holy Land, a field dominated by Gérôme and his followers, satisfied those collectors interested in the mysterious customs of the East. Erotic subjects, if thinly-veiled by a pretense of moral content, such as a theme involving Venus or an exotic harem girl, were acceptable and indeed quite profitable for Bouguereau, Cabanal, and a legion of lesser artists.

American collectors, such as William C. Corcoran of Washington, William T. Walters of Baltimore, and A.T. Stewart and William H. Vanderbilt of New York City, appreciated the beauty of Salon art and collected it with the full confidence that they were acquiring works of proven artistic and financial value. Americans were especially attracted to genre painting, with landscape painting holding a close second.[10] In addition to the appeal of their subject matter, Salon painters had the added advantage of being living painters: an acquisition could be authenticated, a collector could meet the artist and commission a specific, highly customized theme. Often American collectors relied upon art dealers, such as Samuel P. Avery or George A. Lucas, to guide their choices or to introduce them to artists. A dealer's intimate knowledge of the art market and personal contacts with artists enable him to assure his clients that they were receiving the finest works at the best prices, thereby eliminating the mistakes in judgment those less experienced in the market might make. Arnot was acquainted with dealers and, in fact, he may have known Avery quite well as both were members of the same private clubs in New York.[11] He purchased two paintings from Avery's son, a landscape by Sanchez-Perrier (acc. no. 36) and an *animalier* painting by Verboeckhoven (acc. no. 46).[12] However, unlike other collectors of the period, Arnot chose not to rely upon the advice or services of a dealer, preferring instead to select and purchase only those artists and works that appealed to him. Initially, his art purchases were mementos of his travels but as he matured, he gained confidence in his eye and his acquisitions became more informed and assured.

Arnot's collection grew slowly. His first acquisitions were made in Rome in 1869-1870 when he commissioned a marble bust of his father from Chauncey Bradley Ives (acc.

no. 307) and a small version of the popular sculpture *The Wept of Wish-ton-Wish* from Joseph Mozier (acc. no. 308). These sculptors were part of the American colony of artists working in Rome and both were highly acclaimed in the press. Like other American tourists, Arnot visited the artists' studios to acquire some of their work. The selection of Ives to do a portrait bust of Arnot's father seems to be a choice dictated by the desire for prestige rather than personal taste. In particular, Ives was the sculptor most frequently sought out by the many American and Englishmen abroad. He represents a certain level of aesthetic taste of the elite in the 1860s and 1870s.[13] Arnot's respectful and learned appreciation of such celebrated artists suggests that this commission might have been an attempt to persuade his father, if only through flattery, of the investment value of art.

Arnot returned to Italy in the early 1870s and probably during this trip acquired two small genre paintings by A.E. Fabri (acc. 23) and Roberto Rassinelli (acc. no. 24), minor Italian artists working in Rome. These modest works appear to be souvenirs of his travels, much like his 1876 acquisitions in Brussels of another Italian genre scene, this one by Luigi Zuccoli (acc. no. 56), purchased from an exhibition and the first *animalier* painting of the collection, *Interior of a Barn with Sheep* (acc. no. 45), purchased from the artist, Eugène Joseph Verboeckhoven.

His next art purchases were from the Centennial Exposition in Philadelphia in 1876. The Centennial Expositon brought America's technological achievements to the attention of the world and, through the art displayed in Memorial Hall, brought the accomplishments of contemporary foreign artists to America. Arnot apparently was very impressed with the display of German artists and purchased genre paintings by acclaimed masters, Friedreich Peter Hiddeman's *Nobody Was Ever a Master* (acc. no. 58), Sigmund Eggert's *The Village Artist* (acc. no. 64), and Meyer von Bremen's *The Village Gossips*, purchased for his sister Marianna Arnot Ogden. Arnot's taste was later officially endorsed when the Eggert painting was illustrated in the three-volume catalogue entitled *The Masterpieces of the Centennial International Exhibition* while *The Village Gossips* was listed in *The Illustrated History of the Centennial* as one of the more notable pictures by German artists.[14]

By 1879, Arnot's collection grew in scope as evidenced by his contributions to the Loan Exhibition, a month-long cultural extravaganza for the benefit of Elmira's Home for the Aged. In addition to the genre paintings purchased in Philadelphia, he also contributed several new works, including two more *animalier* paintings, Charles-Emile Jacque's *Barn Yard* (acc. no. 9) and Emile van Marcke's *Cattle in a Pool* (acc. no. 8), as well as his first orientalist work, Adolphe Schreyer's *Mid-day Halt* (acc. no. 65), and nine bronzes from his collection. Most of these works were small bronze copies of famous marble sculptures, such as Chaudet's neo-classical work entitled *Amor Catching a Butterfly* (acc. no. 311) and the parlor-sized reproduction of the Venus de Milo (acc. no. 300). Barye's bronze stag (acc. no. 319) was affectionately described in the exhibition catalogue as a reindeer.[15]

In the 1880s and the decades to follow, Arnot collected with purpose and plan, starting with a balanced assortment of Old Masters and progressing to the best in contemporary art. He was less concerned with acquiring Salon works—only six in the collection were actually exhibited in a Salon—than he was that the works be by artists who regularly showed in the Salon and had won numerous awards. Genre painting, both French and German, had the most appeal for him and constitutes over half the collection. It is also clear that the source of his purchasing was especially important to him. Starting in 1882, Arnot almost exclusively bought works from other collections, thereby obtaining such works which had the added luster of previous ownership by a noted connoisseur. Such an association conferred distinction upon the new owner and reconfirmed the quality and desirability of a specific work. Arnot made sure visitors appreciated his efforts in assembling such an impressive collection. In the catalogue of his collection published circa 1900, he included the provenance of each work.[16] Furthermore, sales of private collections were convenient and efficient, enabling a collector to acquire several works within one or two days. Such auctions, though removing much of the risk from acquiring art, did offer the thrill of competition as bidders vied for coveted pieces.

Arnot approached collection sales quite seriously. He studied the contents of the auction prior to the sale and noted in the catalogue which artists or works particularly caught his eye, occasionally commenting on the quality of the work.[17] Though he was not an impulsive bidder, once he was committed to a specific work, he kept bidding until he secured it for his collection and, consequently, he was often criticized for paying exorbitant prices. Such notoriety probably appalled this normally quiet and reserved gentleman from Elmira and, in some sales, Arnot employed an intermediary to do his bidding in

Loan Exhibition had an additional benefit, as the editors of the *Daily Advertiser* (May 31, 1879) noted, in "the bringing together of the inhabitants of our city face to face, the dissolution of clans, clubs, and coteries. . ." as the entire city, not just the wealthy, must support the event to make it a success. A catalogue of the exhibition is in the collection of the Chemung County Historical Society and daily reports of the event were published in the *Daily Advertiser*.

Arnot lent the following works to the exhibition, listed by number in the Loan Exhibition catalogue [followed by AAM acc. no.]: 1722: Real Bronze Figure of Cupid and the Butterfly [acc. no. 311]; 1751: Real Bronze Figure, Mercury [acc. no. 329]; 1780-1: French Soldiers at an early period, real Bronze; 1782: Reindeer, Real Bronze [acc. no. 319]; 1783: Two Soldiers at an early period, Silver Bronze; 181: A Venus, Real Bronze; 1812: Ariadne, Real Bronze; 1813: Sappho, Real Bronze; and 1822: The Venus of Milo, real Bronze [acc. no. 300]. Paintings were separately numbered: 98: The Village Artist (Eggert) [acc. no. 64]; 99: Portrait, General Taylor (Street) [acc. no. 72]; 100: Sheep (Verboeckhoven) [acc. no. 45]; 101: Cattle in Pond (Von Marcke) [acc. no. 8]; 102: The Halt (Schreyer) [acc. no. 65]; 103: The Barnyard (Jacque) [acc. no. 9]; 105: The Peasant's Bride (Zuccoli) [acc. no. 56]; 106: Nobody was Born a Master (Hiddleman [sic]) [acc. no. 58]; 112: Sweep and Maid (Gypad.) [acc. no. 68]; and 113: Morning (Boughton) [acc. no. 28].

16   Arnot's catalogue is a fascinating document both for what it does and does not include. He deliberately chose to limit the catalogue to European paintings, omitting three American paintings and all the sculptures that were in his possession at the time the catalogue was published. Given the lack of personal diaries or travel itineraries, the catalogue is the only record, albeit minimal, of where or from whom Arnot acquired artwork. Unfortunately, much of the information in Arnot's catalogue is suspect and conflicts with known provenance, auction catalogues, published accounts of sales, or the documented exhibition history of a given work. More discouraging is Arnot's references to certain collections that subsequent research has been unable to identify or confirm. These are: a Maynard collection (Hugues Merle, acc. no. 35); a Reid collection (Heinrich Hirt, acc. no. 63); and a Wynkoop collection, sold between 1889 and 1900, (C.-F. Daubigny, acc. no. 2; Gustave Courbet, acc. no. 5; J.-L. Gérôme, acc. no. 12; Carl von Merode, acc. no. 16; Rico y Ortega, acc. no. 22; and Maurice Leloir, acc. no. 25). The 1879 sale of a Spencer collection (C.E. Jacque, acc. no. 9; G.H. Boughton, acc. no. 28; and Adolphe Schreyer, acc. no. 65) is most likely the first sale of Albert Spencer's collection mentioned by Strahan [Shinn], who noted in his 1880 volumes on American collectors that "Mr. Albert Spencer, who has already parted with a fashionable collection, is now accumulating works of higher style. . ." *The Art Treasures of America*, vol. 3, p. 123.

17   The Arnot Art Museum has Arnot's annotated catalogues for the sales of the Hamilton Palace collection, Mary Jane Morgan's collection, and George I. Seney's collection as well as the post-sale results of the Hamilton Palace collection published in book form by Remington and Company, London, 1882. See notes 22, 29, and 33 for specific citations.

Arnot would comment on the quality of the work in very general terms, for example, whether is was "excellent," "fine," or just merely "good."

18 Alexander Hamilton-Douglas (1767-1852) was educated at Christ Church, Oxford, and spent his early years in Italy before assuming his family responsibilities in 1801. He took on the title of Duke of Hamilton in 1819, upon the death of his father. In 1810, he married Susan Euphemia Beckford and together they assembled a large collection of pictures, sculpture, decorative objects, and rare books and manuscripts. Alexander's interest in and knowledge of the arts led to his appointments as trustee of the British Museum and vice president of the Royal Institution for the Encouragement of the Fine Arts in Scotland.

The roots of the Hamilton Palace collection were in the wedding gift from Susan's father, William Beckford (1759-1844), an eccentric aesthete, author of *Vathek* (1786), and builder of the Gothic fantasy "abbey" at Fonthill. Upon his daughter's marriage, Beckford gave the couple choice selections from his famed library and art collection at Fonthill. See *The Dictionary of National Biography*, Oxford University Press.

Descriptions of the Beckford and Hamilton Palace collections prior to their dispersals are found in Gustav Waagen, *Works of Art and Artists in England*, 3 vols. (London: John Murray, 1838; reprint ed. Cornmarket Press, 1970) 2: 257-265; 3: 82-89, 112-131, and *The English as Collectors: A Documentary Chrestomathy*, ed. Frank Herrmann (NY: W.W. Norton and Co., Inc., 1972), pp. 210-219, 348-352.

19 *Illustrated London News*, July 15, 1882.

20 London correspondent, *New York Daily Graphic*, August 16, 1882.

21 *New York Tribune*, July 25, 1882.

The dukes of Hamilton had extensive ties to Scotland; through the years, they accumulated and inherited the titles of Marquis of Douglas and Clydesdale and Earl of Angus, Lenark, and Selkirk. (Alexander, the tenth Duke of Hamilton, believed he was the legitimate king of Scotland. At his death, his body was embalmed, deposited in a sarcophagus imported from the Egyptian Pyramids, and buried in a mausoleum he had erected on the grounds of the Hamilton Palace. See *The Dictionary of National Biography*, Oxford University Press.) The Scottish connections of the dukes of Hamilton may have increased the appeal of the palace collection sale for Arnot. His grandfather was a reasonably prosperous farmer from Perthshire, Scotland before emigrating to the United States in 1801. It has been suggested that one or more of the Arnot ancestors worked for the Hamilton line. One may interpret Matthias Arnot's active presence at the Hamilton Palace collection sale as an example of an American success story, that is, of a first generation American willfully and rather grandly acquiring the possessions of his forebears' lords.

order to retain his anonymity and, perhaps, to prevent the price from rising due to his known ability to pay.

In 1882, Arnot gained international fame and, indeed, some might say infamy, at the sale of the Hamilton Palace collection. Assembled by Alexander, the tenth Duke of Hamilton, the collection of paintings contained many fine works by Dutch, Flemish, English, French, and Spanish masters. Some, however, were believed to be of doubtful authenticity.[18] The twelfth Duke of Hamilton auctioned off the whole lot as a result of his "reckless extravagence" which forced him to sell his grandfather's collection in order to repay his debts.[19] The seventeen-day sale was eagerly anticipated and the bidding was expected to be vigorous. The proceeds of the sale were nearly $2,500,000. Most observers believed the total, though less than half what the Duke needed to pay his debt, was too high and the direct result of extravagant foreign bidders. Americans, whose wealth was believed to derive from questionable sources, were accused of stealing British treasures:

There is complaint here that the Americans are carrying off all the precious antiquities and pictures put upon the market by the Duke of Hamilton's sale. One paper complains that England lost everything of value because the Yankees bid until the prices reached were greater than Englishmen, who make their money in legitimate business, could pay.[20]

Matthias Arnot, in particular, was accused of paying "monstrous sums" and the London correspondent to the *New York Tribune* noted:

An American named Arnot has suddenly become an object of interest in London. He appeared at the Hamilton Sale last week, where he and some other of his compatriots with long purses had been looked for earlier. There was a moment when Mr. Vanderbilt was expected to buy pretty much the entire contents of the palace. Whether any of the great dealers have been acting for unnamed American clients nobody can be quite sure, but the impression is that no formidable competitor from America has had much to do with the bidding prior to Mr. Arnot.[21]

Arnot attended the tenth day of the sale, July 8, 1882, for the auction of Dutch, Flemish, French, and Spanish Old Masters. Though he bid on over sixty paintings, only nineteen were secured, including three works by Jan Brueghel (acc. nos. 38, 39, and 49) and a David Teniers genre scene (acc. no. 41).[22] Two of the more celebrated works he acquired was Murillo's *The Infant Christ Sleeping* (acc. 48), whose £2415 knockdown price (approximately $12,000) was considered "an astonishing price for a picture of this kind," and Claude Lorrain's landscape with Ariadne and Bacchus (acc. no. 32), which was greatly admired although one critic did mention that the painting may have been too closely cleaned in the sky area.[23] The most hotly contested painting was Velasquez's portrait of Philip IV of Spain, the so-called Brown and Silver portrait in the National Gallery in London. Several newspapers described the bidding war between Arnot, M. Gauchez, a French collector, and William Burton, representing the National Gallery and the final winner of the painting, much to the relief of the audience at the auction and British critics.

In 1883, Arnot attended the sale of a portion of the collection assembled by Hinman Barrett Hurlbut (1819-1884), a Cleveland lawyer, banker, and vice president of the Cleveland, Columbus, Cincinnati and Indianapolis railroad. Hurlbut was a founder of the Cleveland City Hospital, endowed a professorship of Natural Sciences in Western Reserve College, and was one of the founders of the Cleveland Museum of Art. Over the years, Hurlbut assembled a collection of American and European works, the latter acquired during his travels to Europe in 1865-1868, again in 1881-1882, and through the services of George A. Lucas and Samuel P. Avery. From the 1883 sale, Arnot acquired six paintings, a selection of Old Masters, such as the Ruysdael landscape (currently attributed to Mancadan; acc. no. 52), and contemporary European works, including the historical genre scene by Lucien-Alphonse Gros from the Salon of 1869 (acc. no. 11).[24]

The next collection to capture Arnot's fancy was the highly celebrated sale of Mary Jane Morgan's art collection, held in New York City in March 1886. Mary Jane Sexton Morgan (? -1885) was the wife of the shipping magnate Charles Morgan. Morgan assembled a large art collection, often using the advice of dealers, such as Knoedler or Avery, and just as often relying upon her own opinions, and she was famous for her willingness to pay high prices for art. The *New York Times* reported on the "not hundreds but thousands" of people who were viewing the collection—daily attendance was cited as between eight and eleven thousand—and attributed the enormous public interest to curiosity about "the breaking up of the Morgan collection . . . the most important event in the art world."[25] A number of America's wealthy and noted collectors, including W.J. Walters, Charles Crocker, and William Rockefeller, attended the sale although many of the collectors preferred art dealers, such as Avery or Knoedler, to present their bids. Arnot also had a representative, L.A. Lanthier, who acquired Ludwig Loefftz's *Money*

Changers (acc. no. 66; originally purchased for Marianna Arnot Ogden) and Pierre Marie Beyle's *Fishing for Sole* (acc. no. 30) during the first night of the sale. The second night brought a head-to-head confrontation between Arnot and C.P. Huntington, the railroad tycoon, over Jehan-George Vibert's *The Cardinal's Menu* (acc. 153): "[The bidding] started at $5,000 and jumped rapidly by thousands until $9,000 was reached, then by hundreds to $12,500, at which price it was secured by Mr. Arnaud (sic)."[26] The *New York Herald* noted that the price given for the Vibert "was extremely high," a criticism repeated by the *New York Times*, however the *Elmira Daily Advertiser* was more impressed with their native son outbidding Mr. Huntington.[27] During the third night of the sale, Arnot entered another heated contest, this time over Ludwig Knaus' *The Hunter's Repast*, a painting he later sold but the acquisition of which put him in competition with some of the greatest collectors and wealthiest men of his day:

[The bidding] was started at $5,000 and Messrs. Avery, Huntington, Chapin, and Crocker bid on it until $12,000 was offered. Then Mr. Chapin dropped out and Mr. Rockefeller, and Mr. Arnaud (sic), of Elmira, came in. They two, with Mr. Avery, kept at it alone after $14,000 was passed, and Mr. Arnaud (sic) kept adding $50 bids to those made for Mr. Rockefeller, until he finally secured the prize with his bid of $16,400, and was greeted with hearty applause for his pertinacity.[28]

By the end of the sale, Arnot had bid on over forty works, acquiring five additional contemporary European genre paintings for his collection.[29]

Two years later, Arnot attended the collection sale of Albert Spencer where he acquired several contemporary French works including a Barbizon landscape by Rousseau (acc. no. 3) and an orientalist work by Benjamin-Constant (acc. no. 19). He also acquired a painting which was to become one of the greater triumphs of his collection, Jules Breton's *Le Soir* (acc. no. 6) which Samuel P. Avery purchased for Spencer from the Salon of 1880.[30] In 1889, James H. Stebbins sold off part of his collection and Arnot picked up two more Salon artists' works, Jules-Emile Saintin's painting *Two Oracles* (acc. no. 10) from the Salon of 1872 and J.L.E. Meissonier's tiny historical genre panel entitled *The Stirrup Cup* (acc. no. 15).

The Seney sale in 1891 was the last major sale Arnot attended. George Ingraham Seney (1826-1893) was a banker and railroad investor. He had an extensive European painting collection, a portion of which was sold in 1885 to cover his debts after his bank failed. For the 1891 sale, Arnot again relied on the use of an intermediary to do his bidding. In fact, two agents were employed, James Graham and J.L. Aiken. Nor was he alone in this practice as the *New York Times* reported:

. . . only a few of those who purchased did their own bidding, the majority preferred to intrust (sic) their buying to art dealers and agents, who were there in great strength to add to their own collections and to fill orders for their customers.[31]

In an article entitled "High Bids for Paintings: Meissonier the Favorite at the Seney Sale Yesterday," the *New York Times* described Graham's successful bidding to obtain *Playing Bowles in the Fosse at Antibes* (acc. no. 14) for his client:

The Meissonier of course brought the highest price . . . It is from the Secretan collection sold in 1889. A round of applause was given when the curtains were pulled aside and disclosed this rare work of art. There were no lack of bids from the start at $5,000. Mr. J. Graham finally secured it for $15,000.[32]

Graham bid on eight other paintings and was successful on two, purchasing Auguste Bonheur's *Morning in the Highlands* (acc. no. 31) and Constant Troyon's *The Red Cow* (acc. no. 7) for his client. On the final night of the sale, Arnot kept his agent J.L. Aiken quite busy bidding on over thirty paintings, though he only secured three works, Ludwig Knaus' *The Old Witch* (acc. no. 60) and *The Child's Funeral* (acc. no. 59) and Diaz de la Peña's *In the Pyrenées* (acc. no. 1).[33]

In the mid-1890s, Matthias Arnot built a picture gallery onto the north side of the family home in order to display his collection in the style and manner that befitted it. As his taste in art was a reflection of his time, so was the manner in which he displayed it. Arnot's gallery is typical, in every respect, of the private art galleries found in the residences of many wealthy Americans of the late nineteenth century. Though grander in conception, the picture galleries of William H. Vanderbilt and A.T. Stewart displayed the same characteristics as the Arnot gallery. The room is rectangular in plan, of moderate size, and monumental height. The corners of the room are set at an angle to the end walls and the ceiling is deeply coved, rising to a large rectangular skylight of white glass panels. The floor is of narrow hardwood boards. The walls are accentuated with a panelled oak dado and one has a fireplace with an ornate Federal Revival oak mantel and decorative tiles for the hearth. The walls are painted a dark red and the coved ceiling a deep yellow cream. In Arnot's time, illumination was by a rectangular pipe framework of gas or

22 The Hamilton Palace collection was sold in five sections over seventeen days in June and July, 1882, at the auction house of Christie, Manson, and Woods, London. Arnot attended the tenth day of the sale, spent £7313.05 (approximately $36,000) and purchased the following works, listed by auction lot number from *Hamilton Palace Collection: Illustrated Price Catalogue* (London: Remington and Co., 1882) [followed by AAM acc. no.]: 1013: Rubens and Wildens, *Milking Time*, a landscape, with peasants and animals [acc. no 42; attributed to Anonymous]; 1022: Vitringa, *Shipping in a Squall*, [acc. no. 55]; 1027: Breughel (sic), *A Fair in a Dutch Village*, on copper [acc. no. 49]; 1028: Rotenhamer (sic) and Breughel, *Apollo, with Venus and Cupids dancing* [acc. no. 38]; 1038: W. Van De Velde, *A Man-of-War in a Storm*, with the artist's signature on the back [acc. no. 51]; 1041: Van Dyck, *Head of Charles II*, when a boy in crimson dress and lace collar [acc. no. 43; attributed to Anonymous]; 1042: Van Balen, *Danäe* [acc. no. 40; attributed to Rottenhammer]; 1045: D. Teniers, *Interior of a Kitchen*, with a peasant in a red cap with feather. . . . Signed. [acc. no. 41]; 1050: A. de Lorme, *Interior of a Church*, with figures and dogs [acc. no. 54]; 1057: Steenwyck, *Lot and his Family leaving Sodom* [acc. no. 37]; 1063: Rotenhamer and Breughel, *Diana and Acteon* [acc. no. 39]; 1065: J. De Mabeuse, *The Labours of Hercules*, a set of eleven small pictures, in ebony frame; 1089: H.B., 1826, *A Man with a Brandy Flask*, Fish & c.; 1105: J. Glover, *A View of Borrowdale*-in watercolors [acc. no. 26]; 1117: Philipe de Champagne, *The Martyrdom of St. Stephen* [acc. no. 33; attributed to Jean-Baptiste, de Champaigne]; 1134: Claude Lorrain, *Ariadne and Bacchus* or more probably Ulysses discovering himself to Nausicaa. . . [acc. no. 32]; 1136: Velasquez, *Portrait of a Youth*, in a hat with feather [acc. no. 47; stolen 1945; tentatively attributed to Van Dyck]; and 1138: Murillo, *The Infant Christ Sleeping*. . . [acc. no. 48]. The works of J. de Mabeuse and H.B. (Henry Barker) were deaccessioned from the permanent collection in the 1970s.

23 *London Times*, July 10, 1882.

24 Arnot acquired the following works from the 1883 sale of Hinman Barrett Hurlbut's collection [followed by AAM acc. no.]: Lucien-Alphonse Gros, *Halt of Cavaliers* [acc. no. 11]; Tetar van Elven, *Street Scene in a Flemish Town* [acc. no. 44]; Jacobus Sibrandi Mancadan, *On the Road to Haarlem* [acc. no. 52; attributed to Jacob Ruysdael when purchased]; Anonymous, *The Mill Pond* [acc. no. 53; attributed to Meindert Hobbema when purchased]; Ferdinand Theodor Hildebrandt, *On the North Sea Coast* [acc. no. 57]; and Luis Riccardo Falero, *The Syrian Music Girl* [acc. no. 69].

I suspect the works Arnot acquired from this collection were probably acquired by Hurlbut after 1878 as none of the works were among those lent by Hurlbut for the 1878 Loan Exhibition in Cleveland. I am indebted to Ann K. Sindelar of the Western Reserve Historical Society, Cleveland, Ohio, and Georgina Gy. Toth of the Cleveland Museum of Art for their research on Hurlbut.

Hurlbut's use of Avery and Lucas as agents is documented in Lucas' diary entries describing the acquisitions of a Hugues Merle painting for Hurlbut in 1874. See Lilian M.C. Randall, *The Diary of George A Lucas: An American Art Agent in Paris, 1857-1909*, 2 vols, (Princeton: Princeton University Press, 1979) 2: 388-389, 391.

25 *New York Times*, March 1, 1886.

26 *New York Times*, March 5, 1886.

27 *New York Herald*, March 5, 1886; *New York Times*, March 6, 1886; and *Elmira Daily Advertiser*, March 5, 1886.

28 *New York Times*, March 6, 1886.

29 Mary Jane Morgan's collection was auctioned during the evenings of March 3-5, 1886, at Chickering Hall, New York City. The preview exhibition was at the American Art Galleries from February 12 until the day of the sale. The sale was under the management of the American Art Association and Thomas E. Kirby of the Association was the auctioneer. Arnot attended all three nights of the sale, spent $26,600, and purchased the following works, listed by auction lot number from *Catalogue of the Art Collection formed by the late Mrs. Mary Jane Morgan* (NY: American Art Association, 1886) [followed by AAM acc. no.]: 4: P.M. Beyle, *Fishing for Sole* [acc. no. 30]; 67: L. Loefftz, *Money Changers* [acc. no. 66; originally purchased for Marianna Arnot Ogden]; 69: B.C. Koek Koek, *Winter in Holland*; 153: J.-G. Vibert, *The Cardinal's Menu* [acc. no. 20]; 173: Emile van Marcke, *Cows in a Pool* [acc. no. 8]; and 189: Ludwig Knaus, *The Hunter's Repast*. The Koek Koek painting and Knaus' *The Hunter's Repast* were later sold by Arnot and were not included in his ca. 1900 catalogue of his collection.

30 The diaries of Avery and Lucas frequently mention a "Spencer" and their activities on his behalf to increase his collection, however, there is some confusion as to the exact identity of the collector. The interpreters of the Lucas diaries attribute all the Spencer references to William Augustus Spencer. The editors of the Avery diaries, on the other hand, cite Albert Spencer in the index. Judging from the works Avery mentions as acquiring for "Spencer," in particular Breton's Salon piece of the 1880, Albert Spencer is the correct identification of the collector. Strahan [Shinn] noted in his 1880 volume that Albert Spencer had recently parted with a noted collection and was "accumulating works of higher style, such as J. Breton's *Evening* (with harvest women stretching themselves or reposing)...." *The Art Treasures of America*, vol. 3, p. 123. See p. 575 of *The Diaries, 1871-1882, of Samuel P. Avery, Art Dealer* for reference to the Breton painting.

31 *New York Times*, February 12, 1891.

32 *New York Times*, February 13, 1891.

32

Picture Gallery, Arnot Art Gallery, 1913.

electric lights. Then as now, paintings were hung "Salon-style," one above the other from the chair railing to the cornice, recalling the appearance of the overcrowded salons exhibitions of the nineteenth century. Arnot also placed especially loved paintings on free-standing easels and displayed several works of sculpture, as well as his Egyptian and Greek artifacts in a curio cabinet.

To coincide with the opening of his art gallery, Arnot published a catalogue in which seventy paintings were listed by artist. He included brief descriptions of the artist's nationality, birth date, and, of particular importance to Arnot, the recent provenance of the work. A few had additional information. For example, Breton's painting was accompanied by a poem and Claude's landscape had a lengthy description of the artist. The slim volume was prefaced with instructions to visitors to the gallery:

> *A talent for any art is rare, but it is given to nearly every one to cultivate a taste for art: only it must be cultivated in earnestness.*
> *The more things thou learnest to know and to enjoy, the more complete and full will be for thee, the delight of living.*   Plato

Arnot's determination to collect art, the best art from the most celebrated collections, is matched only by his desire to impress others with it for more than just its value as evidence of his wealth and refinement. In fact, one is struck by the "public" nature of Arnot's private gallery, as demonstrated by the catalogue and later by the bequest of his gallery to the community. Arnot collected art in part for his own enjoyment but also for the benefit and prestige such culture would bring to his community.

America changed dramatically in the years following the Civil War as the country moved from a predominately rural and agricultural society into an expanding urban and industrial power. Increasing mechanization and mass production of goods, improved transportation and communications, and a growing affluence provided an optimistic vision of America and her future. But modernization was not without a price. Industrialization strained the relations between workers and owners, leading to labor unrest, militant unions, and strikes. The swelling number of immigrants, coming to this country with the promise of a better life, only exacerbated working and middle class fears. Cultural differences, competition for jobs, and unemployment created severe social tensions. The government was of little protection: Tammany Hall in New York City was notorious for its corrupt elected officials who operated out of self-interest rather than public concern. As the disparity grew between those who benefitted from the rapid changes in America and those who were exploited by them, so increased the threat of social unrest and class upheaval. The elite in America's private sector recognized a responsibility, if motivated only out of fear, to aid the victims of America's industrialization and such feelings of paternalistic benevolence resulted in public institutions that changed the fabric of urban life. The foundation of hospitals and charity organizations ministered to the illnesses of the body, while cultural institutions, public education, and civic parks corrected the failings of the soul.[34]

Picture Gallery, Vanderbilt residence, New York, ca. 1880.

Throughout the nineteenth century, some writers promoted culture as the antidote for the problems of modernity. The term "culture" suffers from a lack of clarity. In the nineteenth century, it usually referred to a condition or state of achievement. Critics regularly elevated "high" culture—traditional arts, genteel manners—as the antidote for the degraded sensationalism of "mass" culture, such as serialized fiction in newspapers and popular theatre. High culture was the proper defense against such forces of barbarism.[35] The English writer Matthew Arnold had tremendous influence in America. In *Culture and Anarchy*, published in 1867, he wrote that culture, defined as "sweetness and light," is a universal, ennobling spirit. It had the power to develop the soul and was crucial in the effort to improve the individual and society. He argued against the selfish accumulation of art or its use as "an engine of social and class distinction, separating its holder, like a badge or a title, from other people who have not got it."[36] Charles Dudley Warner, in his article entitled "What Is Your Culture to Me?," published in *Scribner's Magazine* shows the profound influence of Arnold in Warner's stern reminder to his readers that those wealthy enough to appreciate culture had the social responsibility not to hoard it:

It is not an unreasonable demand of the majority that the few who have the advantages of the training of college and university, should exhibit the breadth and sweetness of a generous culture, and should shed everywhere that light which ennobles common things.[37]

Warner went on to note that culture was to be shared "since it is all needed to soften the attritions of common life, and guide to nobler aspirations the strong materialistic influences of our restless society."[38] In his book *The Art Idea*, James Jackson Jarves challenged America's elite to assemble the best of Europe's culture:

Let us even compete with other nations, in inviting to our shores the best art of the world. As soon as it reaches our territory, it becomes part of our flesh and blood. Whither the greatest attraction tends, thither will genius go and make it home.[39]

The aim was twofold: to compensate for America's lack of a strong native cultural tradition by providing quality art to educate and improve American artists but also to expose the general public to symbols of beauty. To Jarves, churches and universities, as well as parks and museums, were "moral reformers," promoting decent behavior, discipline and mutual good will. The Protestant reformer Jonathan Baxter Harrison was less concerned with improving the sensibilities of the general public than he was in protecting property from an unruly mob. In *Certain Dangerous Tendancies in American Life*, published in book form in 1880 after several chapters appeared in the *Atlantic*, Harrison proposed culture as a means of class control:

The people who believe in culture, in property, and in order, that is civilization, must establish the necessary agencies for the diffusion of a new culture. Capital must protect itself by organized activities for a new object—the education of the people.[40]

Far from being a luxury, culture was deemed utilitarian if not essential, as exposure to

33 George I. Seney's collection was auctioned during the evenings of February 11-13, 1891, in the Assembly Room of Madison Square Garden. The preview exhibition was at the American Art Galleries from January 28 until the day of the sale. The sale was under the management of the American Art Association and Thomas E. Kirby of the Association was the auctioneer. Arnot attended all three nights of the sale, spent $42,800, and purchased the following works, listed by auction lot number from *Catalogue of Mr. George I. Seney's Important Collection of Modern Paintings* (New York: American Art Association, 1891) [followed by AAM acc. no.]: 147: Constant Tryon, *The Red Cow* [acc. no. 7]; 171: Auguste Bonheur, *Morning in the Highlands* [acc. no. 31]; 190: J.-L.-E. Meissonier, *Bowl Players in the Fosse at Antibes* [acc. no. 14]; 250: Ludwig Knaus, *The Old Witch* [acc. no. 60]; 280: N.V. Diaz de la Peña, *In the Pyrenées* [acc. no. 1]; and 301: Ludwig Knaus, *The Child's Funeral* [acc. no. 59]. Arnot's agent, J.L. Aiken, also purchased 249: H. LeRolle, *The Homeward Path* and 270: N.V. Diaz de la Peña, *The Virgin and Child* although there is no record of these works in Arnot's collection. Aiken may have bought them for himself, another client, or, if they were purchased by Arnot, they were sold prior to the publication of his catalogue, circa 1900.

34 For a discussion of the use of wealth and culture as a form of social reform and class control in Victorian America, see Alan Trachtenberg, *The Incorporation of America: Culture and Society in the Gilded Age* (NY: Hill and Wang, 1982) and *Victorian Culture in America, 1865-1914*, ed. H. Wayne Morgan (Itasca, IL: F. E. Peacock Publishers, Inc., 1973). The series *The American Culture* (NY: George Braziller, 1970) provides an assortment of primary sources with excellent introductory essays. See vol. 4: *Democratic Vistas, 1860-1880*, ed. Alan Trachtenberg, and vol. 5: *The Land of Contrasts, 1880-1901*, ed. Neil Harris. For an intriguing comparison of the uses of wealth in the 1880s and the 1980s, see Debora Silverman, *Selling Culture* (NY: Pantheon Books, 1986). According to Ms. Silverman, the 1980s are a more appropriate illustration of Veblen's "conspicuous consumption" because in today's world, wealth no longer carries with it the social responsibility to give something back to society.

35 This explanation of culture in its nineteenth-century context was derived from Alan Trachtenberg's introduction in *Democratic Vistas, 1860-1880* and Neil Harris' introduction in *The Land of Contrasts, 1880-1901*.

36 Matthew Arnold's impact on America's intellectual circles is discussed in *Democratic Vistas, 1860-1880*, pp. 16-17.

37 Charles Dudley Warner, "What Is Your Culture to Me?," *Scribner's Magazine* IV (1872): 472.

38 Ibid.

39 James Jackson Jarves, *The Art Idea*, ed. by Benjamin Rowland, Jr. (Cambridge, MA: The Belknap Press of Harvard University Press, 1960), p. 167. Jarves' theories are discussed in Alan Trachtenberg, *The Incorporation of America: Culture and Society in the Gilded Age* (NY: Hill and Wang, 1982), p. 147.

40 Harrison's views are discussed in *Democratic Vistas*, p. 18.

culture made its beholders more sensitive to higher values, more civilized, and, ultimately, more responsible members of society.

The foundation of museums combined the role of art with an elite committed to culture and ready to use their power and resources to support it.[41] The Metropolitan Museum of Art, the Boston Museum of Fine Arts, and the Chicago Art Institute, all founded in the 1870s, promoted this view of culture as a panacea to the ills of modern life. Individual efforts were also successful as many noted collectors of contemporary European art made their collections accessible to the public. In the 1870s, John Taylor Johnston, a railroad tycoon and the first president of the Metropolitan Museum of Art, opened a gallery in his New York City residence to show his collection to the public in the belief that works of art educate and enrich the lives of those who saw them.[42] Also in 1870, the Corcoran Gallery in Washington opened due to the generosity of William C. Corcoran who gave a building fund, endowment, and seventy-nine paintings from his collection for the "encouragement of American Genius."[43] In 1873, Mrs. W.P. Wilstach bequeathed her late husband's collection of Salon art to the city of Philadelphia for an art gallery which, in 1876, became the Philadelphia Museum of Art. She also provided an endowment for acquisitions "always keeping in view the purpose of obtaining objects of the highest skill and beauty, that they may be the source of pleasure and the means of cultivation and refinement of the tastes of the people."[44] These museums, the embodiment of the wealth of the few, were created for the benefit of the many. Admission to the Metropolitan was free on Sundays, the Wilstach bequest insisted the gallery "as soon as practicable shall be gratuitous," and even Arnot's gallery was to be ". . . free and convenient to the public, as may be consistent with the safety and integrity of the property" for ". . . whatever enjoyment or mental or moral elevation such an institution may bestow . . ."[45] If the mission of art was to educate and enlighten the masses, then Salon art was an especially effective and appropriate vehicle: its portrayal of idealized figures, idyllic landscapes, and sentimental stories was easily understood by all beholders. In placing emphasis on refinement, education, and moral elevation, museums were more than emblems of civic pride, they were engines of social change, reforming all who entered to contemplate art's beauty.

Given the context and the role of museums in the late nineteenth century, Arnot's intention to provide the area with an art gallery implies an underlying need. Like other northeast communities, the predominantly rural village of Elmira became a modern industrial city as a result of the Civil War and by the end of the century, Elmira was a progressive, thriving community, the "Queen City" of New York State's Southern Tier.[46] By the 1890s, Elmira was the a communications and transportation hub for the region, with four major railroad lines and sixty-seven passenger trains stopping daily. The Board of Trade, organized in 1879, attracted numerous manufacturing concerns to Elmira, including railroad shops and freight houses, the Elmira Bridge Company, and the American LaFrance Fire Engine Company, as well as lumber and coal yards, tanneries, glue factories, breweries, tobacco factories and woolen mills. Incorporated as a city in 1864, Elmira's population grew from approximately 13,000 in 1865 to over 35,500 by 1900. Outside the workplace, recreation and diversions were plentiful and several hotels in Elmira catered to both tourists and residents. Eldridge Park boasted a lake, picnic grounds, and a casino. Hiking trails and burro rides were available at Rorick's Glen on the Chemung River. There were bicycle clubs, amateur baseball, and youth groups. Special interest groups were organized in response to specific social needs: the Wednesday Morning Club and the Daughters of the American Revolution for women; the YMCA, various service organization and lodges, the Century Club and the City Club for men; and the Country Club for the family. Park Congregational Church set up a lending library in the 1870s and, in 1893, the Steele Memorial Library opened. Several newspapers were available, including two daily papers. The Opera House opened in 1867 to host plays, operas, performers, and lecturers, including Elmira's own Mark Twain.

Elmira was not immune from the problems of modern urban life and by 1890 it was a "city under stress."[47] The influx of new residents, many newly-arrived immigrants from Southern Europe drawn to the area by work on the railroads, contributed to crowded and substandard housing, poverty, and ethnic isolation. Corrupt government, prostitution, gambling, drunkenness, and vagrancy were common complaints by many citizens. Elmira's wealthier inhabitants took matters into their own hands and embarked on programs to reform the conditions of their city. The Women's Committee for Good Government investigated municipal vice and corruption. The privately-funded Industrial School opened in 1877 for vocational training of the poor. In 1888, the Arnot-Ogden Memorial Hospital opened to care for the sick and indigent, while the Home for the Aged and the Orphans Home provided much needed shelter to those unable to care for themselves. In 1876, a progressive state reformatory opened under the guidance of

---

41 For a fascinating study of the use of wealth and culture and its impact on the development of one city, see Helen Lefkowitz Horowitz, *Culture and City: Cultural Philanthropy in Chicago from the 1880s to 1971* (Lexington: University Press of Kentucky, 1976). Neil Harris focuses on Boston in his article "The Gilded Age Revisited: Boston and the Museum Movement," *American Quarterly* 14 (Winter 1962): 545-566.

42 For a discussion of Johnston and his collection, see "Extracts from the Paris Journal of John Taylor Johnston," ed. Katherine Baetjar, *Apollo* 114 (December 1981): 410-417 and Madeleine Fidell Beaufort and Jeanne K. Welcher, "Some Views of Art Buying in New York in the 1870s and 1880s," *The Oxford Art Journal* 5:1 (1982): 48-55. For his relationship to Avery, see *The Diaries, 1871-1882, of Samuel P. Avery, Art Dealer*, pp. lx-lxi.

43 Russell Lynes, *The Tastemakers: The Shaping of American Popular Taste* (NY: Harper and Brothers, 1955; reprint ed. Dover Publications, 1980), p. 62.

44 *Catalogue of the W.P. Wilstach Collection*, ed. by Carol H. Beck (Philadelphia: Commissioners of Fairmont Park and Dunlop Printing Company, 1900), n.p. The Wilstach collection was initially housed in Memorial Hall, the art gallery of the Centennial Exposition, while a new building was erected. In the introduction of the 1900 catalogue of the collection, Ms. Beck cites a passage on Ruskin to explain the high moral purpose of art and the obligation of the wealthy to provide for those less fortunate, secure in the knowledge that, at the very least, future generations will appreciate the effort.

45 In *Maggie: A Girl of the Streets*, published privately in 1893, Stephen Crane includes a description of Maggie and Pete, two of New York's "low life," to quote William Dean Howell's review of the book, visiting the Metropolitan Museum of Art on a Sunday afternoon where Pete "would go to the mummies and moralize over them." *The Portable Stephen Crane*, ed. Joseph Katz (NY: Penguin Books, 1969), p. 33.
Memorandum for the Trustees of the Arnot Art Gallery, p. 1. Arnot provided the trustees of the gallery this memorandum on the methods of administering such an institution, "not for the purpose of dictating, but of suggesting." In this document, he made it explicit how he wished the gallery to function, financially and practically, from acquisition policy to daily hours, but he acknowledged the trustees are ultimately responsible: "I have founded but they must build and administer."

46 Information about the history and development of Elmira were found in the following sources: Ausburn Towner, *History of Chemung County, New York* (Elmira, NY: n.p., 1892); Thomas E. Byrne, *Chemung County: 1890-1975* (Elmira, NY: Chemung County Historical Society, 1976); Michelle Cotton, *Mark Twain's Elmira: 1870-1910* (Elmira, NY: Chemung County Historical Society, 1985); and Cara Sutherland, *"150": A Celebration of Chemung County's Heritage* (Elmira, NY: Chemung County Historical Society, 1986).

Zebulon Brockway who believed rehabilitation and reform of young offenders was possible through vocational training and education. In a similar vein, the Women's Christian Temperance Union established The Anchorage in 1890 as a refuge and vocational school to reform and redeem the area's wayward and unfortunate girls.

These institutions are studies in moral entrepreneurship, funded, managed, and maintained by Elmira's elite to re-establish order and control in their city.[48] The establishment of an art gallery was Matthias Arnot's contribution to and connection with this climate of moral reform. By providing access to art, his gallery was yet another institution predicated on behavior modification, reform, and social control.[49] The collection was an illustration of man's higher achievements and nobler aspirations; intending to educate and uplift all who saw it. Arnot's well-publicized activities to assemble his collection, snatching away coveted works from other famous collectors and collections, would only enhance public curiousity, magnifying their interest in and admiration for their collection. It is not unreasonable to suppose that Arnot, one of Elmira's leading businessmen and the president of the city's largest bank, may have justified the enormous sums of money he spent on art with the knowledge that, in the end, the community would benefit. After all, the goal was not mere acquisitiveness for its own sake or, to quote Thorsten Veblen's famous indictment of this generation, "the conspicuous consumption of valuable goods."[50] Matthias Arnot, his collection, and his 1910 bequest belie such superficial motivations. Certainly he derived great pleasure from the individual works, appreciated their beauty, and felt enriched by their possession and proximity. And, no doubt, he found personal satisfaction and power in the acquisition, outbidding formidable rivals, and capturing a precious treasure. But the greater significance and more profound impact of Matthias Arnot's life was not in the individual masterpiece or even the combined glory of his collection, it was in his determination to bring this art collection to Elmira and to present to the city and the surrounding regions the path of enlightenment and the promise of a better life.

47   Cara A. Sutherland, "The Anchorage: A Case Study in Moral Entrepreneurship," paper written March 1987 for a graduate seminar in history at SUNY-Binghamton. Ms. Sutherland's manuscript discusses The Anchorage as an illustration of Progressive Reform and her research provides valuable insight into the Victorian context and intent underlying many of the institutions established in this period of Elmira's history.

48   As Howard S. Becker points out, "Moral crusaders typically want to help those beneath them to achieve a better status. That those beneath them do not always like the means proposed for their salvation is another matter. But this fact—that moral crusaders are typically dominated by those in the upper levels of the social structure—means that they add to the power they derive from the legitimacy of their moral position, the power they derive from their superior position in society." Howard S. Becker, "Moral Entrepreneurs: The Creation and Enforcement of Deviant Categories," *Deviant Behavior*, ed. Delos H. Kelly (NY: St. Martin's Press, 1979), p. 14.

49   While elevating the educational benefit of art to the masses, Arnot also emphasized to his trustees the need for adequate precautions and security to protect his collection from the public, many of whom would be "careless, thoughtless or ignorant." *Memorandum for the Trustees of the Arnot Art Gallery*, p. 2.

50   Thorstein Veblen, "The Theory of the Leisure Class," published in 1899, is reproduced in *The Portable Veblen*, ed. Max Lerner (NY: Viking Press, 1948), p. 117.

NOTES FOR CATALOGUE ENTRIES

The catalogue entries are grouped in the following categories: Old Masters; nineteenth-century French Salon paintings; nineteenth-century German paintings; nineteenth-century artists of various nationalities; and sculpture. An Index of Artists appears at the end of the catalogue.

The number to the left of the title of each work is the Arnot Art Museum accession number.

Matthias H. Arnot's collection catalogue was published after his picture gallery was completed in the mid-1890s, thus the date of publication for his slim volume is ca. 1900. Any works included in his catalogue are thereby assumed to have been acquired "by 1900" and unidentified or unconfirmed sources of acquisition are listed as in Arnot's catalogue and followed by (?), for example, "Reid collection (?), by 1900."

Dimensions are in inches, height by width (by depth).

Signature and inscription locations are abbreviated LR, LC, and LL (lower right, center and left), CR, CC, and CL (center right, center, and left), and UR, UC, and UL (upper right, center, and left).

ABBREVIATIONS IN BIBLIOGRAPHIC CITATIONS

n.s.	no signature
n.d.	no date
n.p.	no publisher
M.H. Arnot	*Collection of M.H. Arnot* (n.p., [ca. 1900]).
Faison	S. Lane Faison, Jr., *Art Tours and Detours in New York State* (NY: Random House, 1964).
Hamilton 1	*Catalogue of the Collection of the Duke of Hamilton* (London: Christie, Manson, and Woods, 1882)
Hamilton 2	*The Hamilton Palace Collection: Illustrated Price Catalogue* (London: Remington and Co., 1882). [Post-sale review of the collection, prices, and buyers.]
Morgan	*Catalogue of the Art Collection formed by the late Mrs. Mary J. Morgan* (NY: American Art Association, 1886).
Morse	J.D. Morse, *Old Masters in America* (NY: Rand McNally and Co., 1955).
Permanent Collection (1936)	*Permanent Collection of the Arnot Art Gallery* (Elmira, NY: Arnot Art Gallery, 1936).
Permanent Collection (1973)	*Catalogue of the Permanent Collection* (Elmira, NY: Arnot Art Museum, 1973).
Seney	*Catalogue of Mr. George Seney's Important Collection of Modern Paintings* (NY: American Art Galleries, 1891).

THE 1910 BEQUEST OF MATTHIAS H. ARNOT

CLAUDE LORRAIN   French, 1600-1682

32   Ariadne and Bacchus on Naxos (Ulysses Discovering Himself to Nausicaa), 1656

Oil on canvas 30½ x 40⅝ inches
Signed and dated LR: . . . ain (?) 1656

PROVENANCE: According to the inscription on the *Liber Veritatis* drawing (no. 139), executed for "sig francesco Aberiny," 1656; Mr. Furnese, by 1739; Sir William Morrice, by 1742; through English collections to the Earl of Ashburnham, by 1837; Alexander, tenth Duke of Hamilton, 1850 (Ashburnham collection sale); by descent to William, twelfth Duke of Hamilton, 1863; Matthias H. Arnot, 1882 (Hamilton Palace collection sale); by bequest to the Arnot Art Gallery, 1910.

LITERATURE: John Smith, *A Catalogue Raisonné of the Workes of the Most Eminent Dutch, Flemish, and French Painters*, 9 vols. (London: Smith and Son, 1829-1842) 8:266- 267, no. 139 (as "Bacchus and Ariadne or more probably Ulysses Discovering Himself to Nausicaa"); Hamilton 1, p. 147, no. 1134; "The Hamilton Palace Sale," *London Times*, July 10, 1882; Hamilton 2, p. 149, no. 1134; M. H. Arnot, no. 40 (as "Ulysses Discovering Himself to Nausicaa"); Permanent Collection (1936), no. 32; Morse, pp. 29 and 188; Marcel Roethlisberger, *Claude Lorrain, The Paintings*, 2 vols. (New Haven: Yale University Press, 1961) 1:333-335, illus. fig. 233 (as "Coast View of Naxos with Ariadne and Bacchus"); Faison, pp. 186-187, illus.; Marcel Roethlisberger, *Claude Lorrain, The Drawings*, 2 vols. (Berkely and Los Angeles: University of California Press, 1968) 1:298, no. 792; Permanent Collection (1973), p. 115, illus. p. 116; Marcel Roethlisberger and Doretta Cecchi, *L'Opera completa di Claude Lorrain* (Milan: Rizzoli Editions, 1975), no. 208, illus. plate 39 and p. 114, no. 208 (as "Ariadne and Bacchus"); Michael Kitson, *Claude Lorrain: Liber Veritatis* (London: The Trustees of the British Museum, 1978), pp. 136 and 139, no. 139, Appendix C; Pierre Rosenberg, *France in the Golden Age: Seventeenth-Century French Paintings in American Collections* (NY: Metropolitan Museum of Art, 1981), p. 358, illus. no. 11 (as "Ariadne and Bacchus on Naxos"); H. Diane Russell, *Claude Lorrain: 1600-1682* (Washington, D.C.: National Gallery of Art, 1982), no. 45, illus. pp. 25 and 175 (as "Ariadne and Bacchus on Naxos (?)"); "Arnot Painting to be exhibited in Washington," *Elmira Sunday Telegram*, September 26, 1982; John Russell, "Giving Full Due to an Influential Master's Art," *New York Times*, October 24, 1982; H. Diane Russell, *Claude Gellée dit le Lorrain*, trans. Claude Lauriol (Paris: Editions de la Reunion des Musées nationaux, 1983), no. 45, illus. pp. 32 and 191 (as "Ariadne and Bacchus on Naxos (?)").

Claude Gellée, known as Claude Lorrain in his lifetime and now referred to simply as Claude, was born in Champagne and traveled to Rome at an early age, sometime between 1612 and 1620. Apart from brief trips to Naples in 1619-1622 and Nancy in 1625-1626, Claude lived and worked in Rome until his death. By 1630 and after, his success and financial security was assured by steady commissions from Cardinal Bentivoglio, Pope Urban VIII, Spain's Philip IV, princes, Roman dignitaries, and visitors from France. In 1635, he began to keep a register of his paintings in a book of sketches entitled *Liber Veritatis*, now in the British Museum, in an effort to keep track of his works and probably to discourage forgeries.

Claude's fame, great during his lifetime, has scarcely diminished in the years following his death and legions of landscape painters count him as having considerable influence on their work. Inspired by the golden light and delicate scenery of the Roman *compagna*, Claude observed natural phenomenae and the changing effects of light which he organized in paintings of idealized landscapes. Though he often relied upon a narrative theme and animated his scenes with figures, the true subject of his paintings is the landscape with its richly-textured grounds and shimmering bodies of water.

Ariadne and Bacchus on Naxos was completed in 1656 on commission for, according to Kitson, the Roman nobleman Francesco Arberini and is considered to be the first painting by Claude to enter a public collection in the United States. It is a pendant to *Apollo Guarding the Herds of Admetus and Mercury Stealing Them*, 1654, also commissioned by Arberini and now in the collection of Viscount Coke, Great Britain. The exact subject of the Arnot painting has proved difficult to determine. Both the subjects, Ariadne-Bacchus and Ulysses-Nausicaa, were suggested by Smith in 1837, although neither story conforms very comfortably to the visual image. The Ulysses-Nausicaa episode is found in Homer's *Odyssey* VI, while the story of Bacchus and Ariadne appears in Ovid's *Ars amatoria* (1:529-562), *Fasti* (3:459-516), and *Metamorphoses* (8:169-182), Philostratus the Elder's *Imagines* (1:15), and Catullus' *Carmina* (64). Roethlisberger clearly prefers the Ariadne title and Kitson agrees (p. 139), noting Ovid's brief lines from *Metamorphoses* (8:176 f.) may have been the inspiration for this painting illustrating Ariadne, daughter of King Minos, after her desertion by Theseus on the island of Naxos where she was rescued by Bacchus:

> *Ariadne, left all alone, was sadly lamenting*
> *her fate, when Bacchus put his arms around her*
> *and brought her his aid.*

If this attribution is correct then the figure in the small boat is Theseus sailing away, the figure emerging from behind the tree and the bushes at the right is Bacchus, and the seated figure with her hand to her breast is Ariadne who looks toward the tree, startled by Bacchus' approach. Despite the ambiguous iconography, the painting is an illustration of Claude's powers as a brilliant colorist: the deep blue green of the agitated sea; the warm greens and browns of the foliage; and the juxtaposition of Ariadne's white skin and mauve-toned dress against a deep blue cloth.

CLAUDE LORRAIN, Ariadne and Bacchus on Naxos (Ulysses Discovering Himself to Nausicaa); color plate p. 9

JEAN-BAPTISTE DE CHAMPAIGNE   French, b. Brussels, 1631-1681

33   The Stoning of St. Paul, ca. 1667
Oil on canvas 24$^{1}/_{8}$ x 22$^{3}/_{4}$ inches
n.s.

PROVENANCE: Alexander, tenth Duke of Hamilton, by 1852; by descent to William, twelfth Duke of Hamilton, 1863; Matthias H. Arnot, 1882 (Hamilton Palace collection sale); by bequest to the Arnot Art Gallery, 1910.

LITERATURE: Gustav Waagen, *Treasures of Art in Great Britain*, 3 vols. (London: J. Murray, 1854) 1:300 (as Philip de Champagne, "The Martyrdom of St. Stephen"); Hamilton 1, p. 145, no. 1117 (as Philip de Champagne, "The Martyrdom of St. Stephen"); "The Hamilton Palace Sale," *London Times*, July 10, 1882; Hamilton 2, p. 146, no. 1117 (as Philip de Champagne, "The Martyrdom of St. Stephen"); M. H. Arnot, no. 43 (as Philip de Champagne, "The Martyrdom of St. Stephen"); Permanent Collection (1936), no. 33 (as Philip de Champagne, "The Stoning of St. Stephen"); Morse, p. 188; Faison, p. 188, illus.; Permanent Collection (1973), p. 98, illus. (as Jean-Baptiste de Champaigne, "The Stoning of St. Paul"); Pierre Rosenberg, *France in the Golden Age: Seventeenth-Century French Paintings in American Collections* (NY: Metropolitan Museum of Art, 1981), pp. 231 and 348, illus. p. 348, no. 6.

Born in Brussels, Champaigne came to Paris in 1643 where he studied with his uncle, Philippe de Champaigne (1602-1674), who was a founding member of the Académie Royale de Peinture et de Sculpture and whose patrons included Louis XIII and Cardinal Richelieu. In 1658-1659, Jean-Baptiste traveled to Italy to study. After his return to Paris, he was elected to the Académie in 1663 and became a professor the following year, frequently lecturing on Titian, Guido Reni, and Poussin. He enjoyed many royal commissions, including an important role in the decoration of the residences at Versailles, Vincennes and the Tuileries.

He often collaborated with his uncle which resulted in latter-day historians confusing one artist's work with the other's. The Arnot painting is one such example, having been attributed to Philippe until the mid-1960s when it was identified as being by Jean-Baptiste. The subject of the painting was also correctly deciphered at this time as being the stoning of St. Paul rather than St. Stephen. The confusion in iconography is understandable given the resemblance to the latter story in which Stephen was stoned to death by an angry crowd following his famous sermon in Jerusalem in which he proclaimed his vision of seeing Christ in heaven. St. Paul, on the other hand, was in Lystra with St. Barabus where their miraculous cure of a cripple incited the pagan residents of Lystra to make a sacrifice, as they believed the apostles to be Mercury and Jupiter. The apostles prevented the sacrifice by tearing their clothes. The painting appears to be a conflation of the two stories with the Jewish elders inciting the angry crowd to hurl stones at Paul, depicted in torn raiments and huddled on the stone steps beside a Roman temple. Documentation in the Louvre indicates Jean-Baptiste received a commission in 1667 from a society of goldsmiths for a "May," a painting given to Notre Dame Cathedral on May 1, 1667 of the subject "St. Paul Stoned at Lystra" (letter dated June 25, 1968 from Sylvie Beguin, curator, Louvre). The finished commission is now in the collection of the Musée des Beaux-Arts, Marseilles, and the Arnot painting is a sketch or copy made by the artist of the larger painting. Jean-Baptiste's style recalls his admiration for Nicholas Poussin (1594?-1665), in the emphasis on clear delineation of foreground action through complementary poses and a variety of gestures strategically placed across the canvas. Philippe's influence on his nephew is evident in the finished execution and the coldness of the local colors, such as the ivory-yellow tones with pale violet shadows in the figure on the left or, in the cowering saint, the bluish green dress offsetting the pink robe.

WEGERUS VITRINGA   Dutch, 1657-1725

55   Shipping in a Squall, n.d.
Oil on panel 8$^{3}/_{4}$ x 11$^{3}/_{4}$ inches
n.s.

PROVENANCE: Alexander, tenth Duke of Hamilton, by 1852; by descent to William, twelfth Duke of Hamilton, 1863; Matthias H. Arnot, 1882 (Hamilton Palace collection sale); by bequest to the Arnot Art Gallery, 1910.

LITERATURE: Hamilton 1, p. 133, no. 1022; "The Hamilton Palace Sale," *London Times*, July 10, 1882; Hamilton 2, p. 137, no. 1022; M. H. Arnot, no. 33; Permanent Collection (1936), no. 55; Permanent Collection (1973), p. 140.

Vitringa was born in Leeuwarden, Friesland, in the northern part of the Netherlands, where he pursued a successful law career, advancing to the post of advocate of the Frisian high court. He also produced a number of marine views.

JEAN-BAPTISTE DE CHAMPAIGNE, The Stoning of St. Paul; color plate p. 10

WEGERUS VITRINGA, Shipping in a Squall

WILLEM VAN DE VELDE, THE YOUNGER   (attrib.)

50 A Calm on the Dutch Coast, n.d.
Oil on panel 19 1/8 x 27 1/8 inches (irreg.)
n.s.

PROVENANCE: Albert Spencer ; Matthias H. Arnot, 1888 (Spencer collection sale); by bequest to the Arnot Art Gallery, 1910.

LITERATURE: M. H. Arnot, no. 20; Permanent Collection (1936), no. 50.

    Scholars have disputed the attribution of this painting to Willem van de Velde (letters dated June 14, 1968, and June 8, 1973, from Seymour Slive and M. S. Robinson, respectively). Robinson suggests it may be the work of Esias van de Velde (ca. 1590-1630), the brother of Willem van de Velde, the Elder. Esias was a painter during the early realist phase of seventeenth-century Dutch landscapes as was known for his carefully executed details and a concern for atmospheric tones.

WILLEM VAN DE VELDE, THE YOUNGER   Dutch, 1633-1707

51 Man-of-War in a Storm, ca. 1700
Oil on canvas 25 1/8 x 30 1/8 inches
Signed verso UC: W. v. Velde, Y

PROVENANCE: Alexander, tenth Duke of Hamilton, by 1852; by descent to William, twelfth Duke of Hamilton, 1863; Matthias H. Arnot, 1882 (Hamilton Palace collection sale); by bequest to the Arnot Art Gallery, 1910.

LITERATURE: Hamilton 1, p. 135, no. 1038; Hamilton 2, p. 139, no. 1038; M. H. Arnot, no. 23; Permanent Collection (1936), no. 51; Permanent Collection (1973), p. 137, illus.

    Willem van de Velde, the Younger, was the finest marine painter of the seventeenth century. He was born in Leiden and named after his father, Willem van de Velde, the Elder (1611-1693), the noted Dutch marine painter. By 1636, the family had moved to Amsterdam where a second son, Adriaan van de Velde (1636-1672) was baptised. Around 1648, Willem the Younger moved to Weesp where he studied under the marine painter Simon de Vlieger. In 1652, he married Petronella le Maire of Weesp in Amsterdambut separated a year later and, in 1666, he married Magdelena Walraven. Willem the Elder often went on seafaring expeditions with the Dutch Navy in the offical capacity as artist. His sketches of the battles of the Anglo-Dutch wars in 1652-1674 were often transformed by Willem the Younger into oil paintings which combined miscellaneous groups of warring ships in dramatic compositions. In the winter of 1672 or early in 1673, the van de Velde family moved to England, perhaps as a result of the French invasion of the Netherlands, although the excellent opportunity to work for another major maritime nation may have attracted them. They soon became court painters to Charles II, and later, to James II. The van de Veldes were paid both a salary and a commission, Willem the Elder for sketching seafights and Willem the Younger for making paintings of the sketches. The court gave them a studio at the Queens House in Greenwich. In 1694, after the death of his father, Willem the Younger sailed with the English fleet to the Mediterranean. In his later years, Willem the Younger oversaw a large studio of marine artists producing versions, variations and copies of his paintings.

    Man-of-War in a Storm dates to Willem the Younger's English period and illustrates an English ship caught in a gale. (Robinson notes the style of the painting appears to date it near 1700 though the design of the ship is probably closer to 1675. Letter dated June 8, 1973, from M. S. Robinson.) Van de Velde's concern for accuracy is evident in his strict recreation of the ship, its design, rigging, and decoration. He was also interested in its position and orientation on the choppy waters and the partial yet dramatic illumination of the ship in the dwindling light. Such technical concerns of a marine painter were outlined by Willem the Younger on one of his drawings:

> *There is much to observe in beginning a painting; whether you will make it mostly brown or mostly light; you must attend to the subject, as the air and the nature of its color, the directions of the sun and wind, whether the latter be strong or moderate, are to be chosen as may seem best. Then the sketching of the ordinance or ships under sail . . .* (quoted in Jakob Rosenberg, Seymour Slive, and E. H. ter Kuile, *Dutch Art and Architecture: 1600-1800*, NY: Penguin Books, 1979, pp. 285-286).

    Some scholars question whether marine paintings, such as those by van de Velde, were merely straightforward records of ships and naval battles or if, like genre paintings, they hold greater symbolic meanings. Simon Schama notes that in Dutch literature the ship embodies the medieval connotation of the mother church, as well as implying the *Narrenschiff*, the Ship of Fools, and the humanist image of Ship of State. All were "garbled together to make a composite metaphor for the Dutch community, set adrift on the 'great historical ocean'." Schama suggests Dutch marine paintings may be read in a similar fashion (Simon Schama, *The Embarrassment of Riches*, NY: Alfred A. Knopf, 1987, p. 31).

WILLEM VAN DE VELDE, THE YOUNGER, A Calm on the Dutch Coast

WILLEM VAN DE VELDE, THE YOUNGER, Man-of-War in a Storm; color plate p. 14

ANTHONIE DE LORME   Dutch, ca. 1610-1673

54 Interior of a Church, 1667
Oil on canvas 55¼ x 43 inches
Signed and dated LL: A. de Lorme 1667

PROVENANCE: Alexander, tenth Duke of Hamilton, by 1852; by descent to William, twelfth Duke of Hamilton, 1863; Matthias H. Arnot, 1882 (Hamilton Palace collection sale); by bequest to the Arnot Art Gallery, 1910.

LITERATURE: Hamilton 1, p. 136, no. 1050; "The Hamilton Palace Sale," *London Times*, July 10, 1882; Hamilton 2, p. 140, no. 1050; M. H. Arnot, no. 27; Permanent Collection (1936), no. 54; Permanent Collection (1973), p. 101, illus. p. 102.

During the seventeenth century, a large group of Dutch artists specialized in paintings which illustrated the power and beauty of architectural forms. Church subjects, particularly Dutch Protestant churches with their whitewashed interiors and minimal decoration, often conveyed a mystical ambience from the painter's depiction of the spatial grandeur and the interplay of light and shadow. The number of artists working in this genre indicates there was a ready market in the Netherlands' art buying public, many of whom purchased architectural paintings to decorate their homes, although some paintings were commissioned by the subject churches. In the first part of the century, architectural views and interiors were not always of actual structures but rather were exercises in perspective, intended to demonstrate the artist's skill in recreating various architectural features. In the 1630s, Pieter Jansz. Saenredam (1597-1665) emphasized an objective approach with an archeological correctness which paved the way for more realistic and less fanciful architectural paintings. Emanuel de Witte (1616/1618-1692) also worked in this vein. Inspired by actual churches in Amsterdam, he would rearrange certain architectural motifs to heighten the spatial effect, often using figures to give scale and to animate the interior. Lending color and action to the massive space, these figures usually embodied specific themes and provided an iconographic content which was not lost on contemporary viewers.

Anthonie de Lorme was an architectural painter in the style of de Witte and Saenredam. De Lorme was the pupil of the architectural painter Jan van Vucht and he was also influenced by the imaginary interiors and perspective views of Bartholomeus van Bassen. In the 1640s, de Lorme painted a number of fanciful church interiors but, after 1652, his approach was marked by direct observations of actual spaces and he began producing portraits of St. Laurens Church in Rotterdam. The dramatic recession in space of *Interior of a Church* illustrates the view across the nave into the south ambulatory of St. Laurens Church. De Lorme's cool, limited palette of greys and browns captures the luminous interior of the church. The figures and animals in the foreground have been tentatively interpreted by one scholar as a "wedding scene" between the couple walking away arm in arm, while the "witness" walks behind and directs the viewer's attention to the couple. The dogs in the foreground further amplify this theme. They warily eye one another as prelude to establishing their own relationship. (Letter dated April 21, 1988, from Jan Lopez. Ms. Lopez notes the "meaning" of de Lorme's painting is somewhat ambiguous and he seems more concerned with the topographical rendering rather than the iconographic reading.)

ANTHONIE DE LORME, Interior of a Church; color plate p. 15

HENDRIK VAN STEENWYCK, THE ELDER   Dutch, ca. 1550-1603

37 Lot and His Family Leaving Sodom, n.d.
Oil on panel 7 x 8⁷/₁₆ inches
n.s.

PROVENANCE: Alexander, tenth Duke of Hamilton, by 1852; by descent to William, twelfth Duke of Hamilton, 1863; Matthias H. Arnot, 1882 (Hamilton Palace collection sale); by bequest to the Arnot Art Gallery, 1910.

LITERATURE: Hamilton 1, p. 137, no. 1057; Hamilton 2, p. 141, no. 1057; M. H. Arnot, no. 29; Permanent Collection (1936), no. 37; Permanent Collection (1973), p. 138.

    Hendrik van Steenwyck, the Elder, was a Protestent from the Dutch town of Steenwyck who fled the country to escape religious persecution. He settled in Aix-la-Chapelle and while there became the pupil of Hans de Vries. In 1577, he went to Antwerp where he attained the title of Master in the painter's guild. Political pressures again forced him to flee and, in 1856, he settled in Frankfort. Hendrik specialized in perspective and architectural studies, painting scenes of church interiors, palaces and other buildings. He also achieved notoriety for his skill at rendering torch light effects.

    Lot and His Family Leaving Sodom is an intriguing choice of subject from an artist who similarly was forced to flee his home. As described in Genesis (19:1-28), two angels arriving at the gates of Sodom were welcomed by Lot and given hospitality for the night. A band of Sodomites demanded Lot turn over the angels but Lot, hoping to divert their attentions, offered them his daughters instead. God intervened, blinded the Sodomites and drove them away. The angels then warned Lot that he must flee before God destroyed the lawless city. Hendrik illustrates Lot, led by a blue-robed angel and followed by his two daughters and the second angel, escaping from the city already engulfed in flames. Lot's wife stands in front of the city gate in the background at left, observing the destruction and just prior to her turning into a pillar of salt. *Lot and His Family Leaving Sodom* exhibits Hendrik's talent for capturing the flickering light of flames, here the destructive fire of Divine wrath, the red and white of the fire illuminating the night sky made darker by the rising columns of smoke.

HENDRIK VAN STEENWYCK, Lot and His Family Leaving Sodom

JACOBUS SIBRANDI MANCADAN   Dutch, ca. 1602-1680

52 Friesland, n.d.
Oil on panel 16⅛ x 26 inches
Monogrammed LL: JM

PROVENANCE: Hinman Barrett Hurlbut; Matthias H. Arnot, 1883 (Hurlbut collection sale); by bequest to the Arnot Art Gallery, 1910.

LITERATURE: M. H. Arnot, no. 44 (as Ruysdael, "On the Road to Haarlem"); Permanent Collection (1936), no. 52 (as Ruysdael, "On the Road to Haarlem"; Morse, pp. 152 and 188; Permanent Collection (1973), p. 117, illus. (as Mancadan, "Friesland").

    Arnot purchased this work in the belief that it was by Jacob van Ruisdael (ca. 1628-1682). This attribution was disputed by Seymour Slive who, on the basis of style, suggested the lesser known artist Jacobus Sibrandi Mancadan, an attribution confirmed by the discovery of Mancadan's monogram at the lower left (letter dated June 14, 1968 from Seymour Slive).

    Mancadan came from Leeuwarden, the capital of Friesland, a lordship in northern Netherland governed by the Hapsburg sovereign. There is some question about his training. He may have studied with Lambert Jacobsz in Leeuwarden or Moyses van Uyttenbroeck in The Hague, or he may have been self-taught, as he began painting late in life. Mancadan worked as a government official and was elected burgomaster of Franeker in 1637 and of Leeuwarden in 1645. As an artist, Mancadan displayed an idiosyncratic palettte, preferring the warm colors of browns, ochres, yellows, rose and greens. Most of his landscapes are idealized Italianate scenes with decaying classical ruins, picturesque rocks, and gnarled trees. Rare in his *oeuvre* are paintings of the Dutch countryside, such as *Friesland* in the Arnot collection. Mancadan owned a farm in the southeastern corner of *Friesland* which gave him the opportunity to observe nature and men at work on the land. Friesland emphasizes the flatness of the Dutch countryside with an extreme one-point perspective view of a road stretching from the foreground to the distant background on the horizon. Several figures walk or ride in carts along the road, a few others work in the field at the right. Mancadan's work exhibits characteristics of the second period of seventeenth-century Dutch landscape painting, the tonal phase in which the realistic impression of nature was emphasized over the human presence. Central to this approach was the delicate handling of the partially overcast sky and the greyish-green tonality of the landscape to suggest the humid Dutch environment.

JACOBUS SIBRANDI MANCADAN, Friesland

JAN BRUEGHEL, THE ELDER   Flemish, 1568-1625

49 A Flemish Fair, 1613
Oil on copper 9^{11}/$_{16}$ x 14^{3}/$_{4}$ inches
Signed and dated LL: Brueghel 1613

PROVENANCE: Alexander, tenth Duke of Hamilton, by 1852; by descent to William, twelfth Duke of Hamilton, 1863; Matthias H. Arnot, 1882 (Hamilton Palace collection sale); by bequest to the Arnot Art Gallery, 1910.

LITERATURE: Hamilton 1, p. 133, no. 1027 (as Brueghel, "A Fair in a Dutch Village"); "The Hamilton Palace Sale," *London Times*, July 10, 1882; Hamilton 2, p. 138, no. 1027 (as Brueghel, "A Fair in a Dutch Village"); M. H. Arnot, no. 3 (as B. Breenberg, "A Dutch Fair"); Permanent Collection (1936), no. 49 (as B. Breenberg, "A Dutch Fair"); Morse, p. 188; Faison, pp. 188-189, illus.; Permanent Collection (1973), p. 95, illus. p. 96 (as Brueghel, "A Flemish Fair"); Klaus Ertz, *Jan Brueghel de Altere (1568-1625): Die Gemalde mit kritishem Oeuvrekatalog* (Cologne: DuMont Buchverlag, 1979), pp. 220-221 and 602, no. 270, illus. p. 220 and plate 277 (as Brueghel, "Landscape with Old Market").

    Jan Brueghel, the Elder, was known as Velvet-, Flower-, or Paradise-Brueghel for his meticulously detailed velvety-textured landscapes and paintings of flowers and fruits. He was the son of Pieter Brueghel, the Elder (1528-1569), the head of a dynasty of artists, whose rustic genre scenes brought him international renown and the title "Peasant-Brueghel." After his father's death, Jan was taken to live with his grandmother, Marie Bessemers, whom Carel van Mander records as having taught watercolor painting to Jan prior to his training with Pieter Goetkint of Antwerp. Around 1589, he traveled to Italy by way of Cologne, arriving in Naples in 1590. In 1592-1594, he worked in Rome for Cardinal Federigo Borromeo and whom he followed to Milan when the Cardinal was appointed Archbishop in 1595. He returned to Antwerp in 1596, became Master of the Antwerp painters' guild, the Guild of St. Luke, and was named Dean of the guild in 1602. His reputation soon brought him financial success, steady patronage, and titles and favors from the court of Archduke Albert and the Infanta Isabella, including his 1610 appointment as court painter. Brueghel was second only to Rubens in his standing in the Flemish art world of the seventeenth century.

    Brueghel's panoramic landscapes link the late sixteenth-century tradition of landscape painting, which incorporated a bird's-eye view, a high horizon, and an emphasis on vertical and oblique elements, with the seventeenth-century tradition, emphasizing the horizontality of the landscape which directs the viewer's attention from the foreground to the distant background by juxtaposing light and dark spaces. In fact, Brueghel's approach to landscape painting led Klaus Ertz to suggest the artist was the forerunner of Dutch tonal landscape painting and a significant influence on its development as a result of his 1613 trip to Holland (Klaus Ertz, *Jan Brueghel, the Elder*, London: Brod Gallery and Klaus Ertz, 1979, pp. 9 and 13). *A Flemish Fair* is set in a village on the banks of a canal. At the extreme right is the village church and another village is barely visible in the far background in the center of the painting. In the foreground, a crowd of villagers, arriving by foot, by boat and by cart, gather together to trade gossip and to barter their livestock and other goods. The influence of Jan's father Pieter is evident in the younger Brueghel's observation of rustic customs but Jan's emphasis is on the decorative rather than the expressive quality of peasant motifs. Bright blues, reds, and greens of the clothing are scattered throughout the scene and their clarity is in sharp contrast to the more tonal and atmospheric treatment of the landscape; browns in the foreground progress to greens and blues as one nears the vanishing point in the center of the painting. Brueghel's meticulous technique is evident in his treatment of the architecture with its clearly defined bricks and shimmering glass, the individualized leaves on the trees, and the delicate delineation of animal fur.

JAN BRUEGHEL, THE ELDER, A Flemish Fair; color plate p. 11

JAN BRUEGHEL, THE ELDER Flemish, 1568-1625 and
JOHANN ROTTENHAMMER German, 1564-1625

38 Venus and Apollo, Putti Dancing, ca. 1595
Oil on copper 11$^{1}/_{8}$ x 8$^{1}/_{8}$ inches
n.s.

PROVENANCE: Alexander, tenth Duke of Hamilton, by 1852; by descent to William, twelfth Duke of Hamilton, 1863; Matthias H. Arnot, 1882 (Hamilton Palace collection sale); by bequest to the Arnot Art Gallery, 1910.

LITERATURE: Hamilton 1, p. 133, no. 1028; "The Hamilton Palace Sale," *London Times*, July 10, 1882; Hamilton 2, p. 138, no. 1028; M. H. Arnot, no. 21; Permanent Collection (1936), no. 38; Faison, p. 189; Permanent Collection (1973), p. 97, illus.

    Brueghel stood at the beginning of a long line of artists. His first marriage to Elisabeth de Jode in 1599 resulted in two children, Jan II who painted in the style of his father and who himself was both father and grandfather to artists, and Paschasia who later married the artist Jan van Kessel. Brueghel's second marriage in 1605 to Katharina van Marienburg produced eight children, including a daughter Anna who later married the artist David Teniers, the Younger (see acc. no. 41). Brueghel's extensive friendships frequently led to collaborations with other artists: Peter Paul Rubens, another court favorite, occasionally painted figures in some of Brueghel's pictures, as did other Flemish artists such as Hendrik van Steenwyck, the Younger, Hendrik van Balen, Frans Francken II, and Josse de Momper.
    The German artist Johann Rottenhammer worked with Brueghel when the two were in Rome. Rottenhammer was born in Munich where he studied under Hans Donauer I from 1582 to 1588. The following year he traveled to Rome where he associated with the group of Northern painters working there, including Brueghel and Paul Bril. From 1596 until 1606, Rottenhammer lived in Venice where his small religious and mythological pictures brought him the steady patronage of Cardinal Borromeo, the Duke of Mantua, and Emperor Rudolf II. In 1606, he returned to his native country to work, settling in Augsberg.
    Around 1595, when both were in Rome, Brueghel and Rottenhammer collaborated on the two mythological paintings on copper in the Arnot collection, Rottenhammer painting the figures to animate Brueghel's landscapes. In *Venus and Apollo, Putti Dancing*, Apollo, the Sun-god and patron of the arts, plays a viol while a circle of putti dance. Venus, the goddess of Love, stands to the side amid her attributes, roses and a pair of doves in the tree above her head. Two flying putti shower flowers and hold aloft an hour-glass, suggesting the transitory nature of such earthly pleasures. Brueghel's delicate landscape is composed of distinct planes receding into space: brown foreground, green middleground and blue background. Alternating zones of light and dark draw the viewer's eye into the distant background.

JAN BRUEGHEL, THE ELDER Flemish, 1568-1625 and
JOHANN ROTTENHAMMER German, 1564-1625

39 Diana and Acteon, ca. 1595
Oil on copper 10$^{5}/_{8}$ x 13$^{15}/_{16}$ inches
n.s.

PROVENANCE: Alexander, tenth Duke of Hamilton, by 1852; by descent to William, twelfth Duke of Hamilton, 1863; Matthias H. Arnot, 1882 (Hamilton Palace collection sale); by bequest to the Arnot Art Gallery, 1910.

LITERATURE: Hamilton 1, p. 138, no. 1063; Hamilton 2, p. 138, no. 1063. M. H. Arnot, no. 12; Permanent Collection (1936), no. 39; Permanent Collection (1973), p. 95, illus. p. 97.

    Diana and Acteon illustrates a passage from Ovid's *Metamorphoses* (3:138-253) in which the young prince Acteon, hunting in the forest, accidentally stumbles upon the forest clearing where Diana, the virgin goddess of the Hunt, is bathing with her companions. To punish him for glimpsing divine nudity, Diana turns him into a stag, whereupon he is chased and destroyed by his own hounds. Brueghel and Rottenhammer chose to depict the moment at which Acteon, in the clearing off to the right and with one of his dogs at his heels, discovers Diana who stands at the left, unaware she is being watched as she drapes a pink cloak around her shoulders. Her attendants are grouped around her in various stages of their toilet—disrobing, bathing, combing their hair. Rottenhammer's traditional format counterbalances the poses and profiles of the heavy and somewhat awkward attendants so they surround and embrace the more idealized beauty of Venus, her significance underscored by the standing figure at right, whose outstretched arm directs the viewer's gaze to the goddess.

JAN BRUEGHEL, THE ELDER and JOHANN ROTTENHAMMER, Venus and Apollo, Putti Dancing; color plate p. 12

JAN BRUEGHEL, THE ELDER and JOHANN ROTTENHAMMER, Diana and Acteon

DAVID TENIERS, THE YOUNGER   Flemish, 1610-1690

41   Interior of a Kitchen, n.d.
Oil on panel 10 x 13$^{1}/_{2}$ inches
Signed LR: D. TENIERS f

PROVENANCE: Alexander, tenth Duke of Hamilton, by 1852; by descent to William, twelfth Duke of Hamilton, 1863; Matthias H. Arnot, 1882 (Hamilton Palace collection sale); by bequest to the Arnot Art Gallery, 1910.

LITERATURE: Hamilton 1, p. 135, no. 1045 (as "Interior of a Kitchen"); "The Hamilton Palace Sale," *London Times*, July 10, 1882; "London Midsummer Gossip," *New York Daily Graphic*, August 16, 1882; Hamilton 2, p. 139, no. 1045 (as "Interior of a Kitchen"); M. H. Arnot, no. 10 (as "Interior of a Dutch Tavern"); Permanent Collection (1936), no. 41 (as "Interior of a Dutch Kitchen"); Morse, p. 188; Faison, p. 189; Permanent Collection (1973), p. 134, illus. p. 135; Jennifer W. Graham, "Building a Treasure," *Horizon* (June 1986):19, illus.

David Teniers, the Younger, like his father-in-law Jan Brueghel (acc. nos. 38, 39, and 49), was from a large family of painters. Born in Antwerp, he initially trained with his father, David Teniers, the Elder (1582-1649), an art dealer who also painted religious and mythological subjects and peasant genre. In 1633, David Teniers, the Younger, became a Master in the painters' guild and eleven years later he was appointed Dean. His 1637 marriage to Brueghel's daughter Anna brought him in contact with a wide circle of artists, including Rubens, van Balen, and two generations of Brueghel painters. In 1647, his reputation for genre painting led to his appointment as court painter to Archduke Leopold Wilhelm and, in 1651, he moved to Brussels where he assumed the role of curator for the Archduke's picture gallery. In the 1660s, he was instrumental in building patronage of the Antwerp Academy by King Philip IV of Spain. Teniers' meticulously finished scenes of peasant genre brought the artist financial success and a wide circle of followers and imitators in his own country as well as by Dutch and other foreign artists.

Teniers' genre scenes are invested with his superb sense of color and an observant eye for variety in the textures and appearances of everyday objects. *Interior of a Kitchen* depicts an assortment of peasants enjoying simple pleasures. The seated man in the foreground elevates his drinking glass and holds a smoking pipe in his other hand. A tendril of exhaled smoke dissolves in the air. Next to him sits a woman, her hands busy folding a paper. In the back, beside the large fireplace, men play cards, watched by two others standing nearby. Teniers' masterful control of color is illustrated by his handling of green tones, ranging from a rich blue-green of the woman's dress and the emerald tones of the man's pants to the grey-green walls and the pale blue tones of the smoking fire, the ensemble set off by the man's red cap and the orange of the fire. Teniers fills the composition with a multitude of objects to show his skill at rendering, for example, the sparkling, smooth surface of the glazed brown pottery which contrast with the rougher surface of the white jug in the foreground. Scholars of seventeenth-century genre painting have demonstrated that these works are more than visual delights to charm the eye; the emphasis on realism is consciously selective and often implies a moralizing theme or serves as an allegory of the human senses. In this light, Teniers painting may be read as containing specific references to taste (drinking), smell (smoke) and sight (playing cards).

JOHANN ROTTENHAMMER   German, 1564-1625

40   Jupiter in a Shower of Gold Descending into the Brazen Tower to Danäe, ca. 1600-1606
Oil on copper 7$^{5}/_{16}$ x 11$^{1}/_{16}$ inches
Signed LR: J. Rottenhammer F. in. Venetia / 16

PROVENANCE: Alexander, tenth Duke of Hamilton, by 1852; by descent to William, twelfth Duke of Hamilton, 1863; Matthias H. Arnot, 1882 (Hamilton Palace collection sale); by bequest to the Arnot Art Gallery, 1910.

LITERATURE: Hamilton 1, p. 135, no. 1042 (as Van Balen, "Danäe"); Hamilton 2, p. 139, no. 1042 (as Van Balen, "Danäe"); M. H. Arnot, no. 25 (as Van Balen, "Jupiter in a shower of Gold descending into the Brazen Tower to Danäe"); Permanent Collection (1936), no. 40; Permanent Collection (1973), p. 129, illus. p. 130 (as by Rottenhammer).

Prior to 1965, this painting of Danäe was ascribed to Hendrik van Balen (1575-1632), a Flemish artist of religious and mythological subjects and who, like Rottenhammer, frequently collaborated with Jan Brueghel. Upon conservation treatment, Rottenhammer's signature was uncovered at the lower right with the inscription "F. in. Venetia." The date was only partially recovered but it indicates the painting dates to the artist's last six years in Venice, 1600-1606.

Danäe was a popular mythological subject for painters. It offered the opportunity to portray the female nude while implying the theme of chastity and the impregnation of a virgin through divine intervention. As a result, Danäe came to be considered a prefiguration of the Annunciation. Danäe's father, the king of Argos, is foretold his daughter's son would kill him whereupon he locks Danäe in a bronze tower to keep her suitors away. Jupiter, however, enters the tower in the form of golden rain. Rottenhammer depicted Danäe reclining on her luxurious bed while from above, Jupiter descends in a shower of gold coins. Danäe is attended by Cupid, who looks up to the heavens and a woman whose stunned amazement of the mystic event does not prevent her from collecting the gold coins on a platter. Rottenhammer's debt to the paintings of the sixteenth-century Venetian artists Giorgione and Titian is apparent in the fleshy, rounded body of Danäe and her frank gaze out to the viewer which supplies an erotic undercurrent to the painting.

DAVID TENIERS, THE YOUNGER, Interior of a Kitchen; color plate p. 13

JOHANN ROTTENHAMMER, Jupiter in a Shower of Gold Descending into the Brazen Tower to Danäe

SCHOOL OF MURILLO   Spanish, 17th century

48 The Infant Christ Sleeping, ca. 1680-1700
Oil on canvas 20⁷/₈ x 26¹/₂ inches
n.s.

PROVENANCE: William Beckford; by gift to Alexander, tenth Duke of Hamilton, 1810; by descent to William, twelfth Duke of Hamilton, 1863; Matthias H. Arnot, 1882 (Hamilton Palace collection sale); by bequest to the Arnot Art Gallery, 1910.

LITERATURE: Gustav Waagen, *Treasures of Art in Great Britain*, 3 vols. (London: J. Murray, 1854) 3:301 (as Murillo, "The Infant Christ Sleeping"); Hamilton 1, p. 148, no. 1138 (as Murillo, "The Infant Christ Sleeping"); "The Hamilton Palace Sale," *London Times*, July 10, 1882; "The Hamilton Palace Sale," *Illustrated London News*, July 15, 1882; Hamilton 2, p. 150, no. 1138 (as Murillo, "The Infant Christ Sleeping"); "London Midsummer Gossip," *New York Daily Graphic*, August 16, 1882; Charles B. Curtis, *Velasquez and Murillo* (NY: J.W. Bouton, 1883), p. 248 (as by Murillo); M. H. Arnot, no. 41 (as by Murillo); *Elmira Sunday Telegram*, January 9, 1923, illus.; Permanent Collection (1936), no. 48 (as by Murillo). Morse, pp. 117 and 188; *Elmira Sunday Telegram*, March 30, 1958, illus.; Permanent Collection (1973), p. 123, illus. (as by Murillo); Diego Angulo Iñiguez, *Murillo: Catalogo Critico*, 3 vols. (Madrid: Espasa-Calpe, S.A., 1981) 2:423, no. 1272.

This painting has generated some confusion with regard to its subject and author. The image of a child holding a staff while asleep on a rock was identified by Waagen as St. John the Baptist. Later scholars, as a rule, prefer to label this work as the Infant Christ. The ethereal image in the background of two angels rounding up sheep prefigured Christ's later role as a shepherd to the flock. As early as the mid-nineteenth century, doubt was placed on the attribution of this painting to Bartolome Murillo (Spanish, 1618-1682). More recently, Angulo Iñiguez suggested the work was from Murillo's School or by an independant follower, citing Cornelius Schut (Flemish, 1629-1685) as a possibility. Jonathan Brown noted the most accurate, albeit somewhat awkward, description of the subject is "Christ Child as Good Shepherd Sleeping while Angels Tend His Flock." Brown agreed with Iñiquez's School of Murillo attribution and added the dates ca. 1680-1700 (letter dated October 9, 1988 from Jonathan Brown).

This particular painting has also been the focus of several inaccuracies about Matthias Arnot, most notably that he dramatically outbid agents of the British government when the painting was offered at the sale of the Hamilton Palace collection, Arnot paying the extravagent sum of $40,000 in order to call the painting his own. In truth, Arnot paid £2415 (then worth approximately $12,000), which was indeed a fabulous sum for what many contemporary accounts asserted was a painting of dubious attribution, but which must have been hotly contested nonetheless, given the high hammer price. (The $40,000 figure was probably taken from Arnot's total expenditure of £7313, or approximately $36,000, for the eighteen works he acquired at the Hamilton Palace sale). Furthermore, Arnot's legendary battle with the British agents was not for this painting, but rather for the full-length portrait of Philip IV by Velasquez, which drew strong bidding action from Matthias Arnot, M. Gauchez, a French collector, and William Burton, the representative of London's National Gallery and the successful bidder.

SCHOOL OF MURILLO, The Infant Christ Sleeping

SIMONE STONE (attrib.)   Flemish (?)

43 Head of Charles II, When a Boy
after Anthony van Dyck
Oil on canvas 15⁵/₈ x 13⁵/₁₆ inches
n.s.

PROVENANCE: Alexander, tenth Duke of Hamilton, by 1852; by descent to William, twelfth Duke of Hamilton, 1863; Matthias H. Arnot, 1882 (Hamilton Palace collection sale); by bequest to the Arnot Art Gallery, 1910.

LITERATURE: Gustav Waagen, *Treasures of Art in Great Britain*, 3 vols. (London: J. Murray, 1854) 2:428 (as by van Dyck); Hamilton 1, p. 135, no. 1041 (as by van Dyck); "The Hamilton Palace Sale," *London Times*, July 10, 1882; Hamilton 2, p. 139, no. 1041 (as by van Dyck); M. H. Arnot, no. 7 (as by van Dyck); Permanent Collection (1936), no. 43 (as by van Dyck); Morse, pp. 66 and 188; *Christian Science Moniter*, January 7, 1959, illus.; Permanent Collection (1973), p. 134 (as by Simone Stone, attrib.).

ANONYMOUS

42 The Farm at Laeken (Milking Time)
after Peter Paul Rubens and Jan Wildens
Oil on panel 21⁷/₁₆ x 31⁷/₈ inches
n.s.

PROVENANCE: Alexander, tenth Duke of Hamilton, by 1852; by descent to William, twelfth Duke of Hamilton, 1863; Matthias H. Arnot, 1882 (Hamilton Palace collection sale); by bequest to the Arnot Art Gallery, 1910.

LITERATURE: Hamilton 1, p. 132, no. 1013 (as Rubens and Wildens, "Milking Time"); "The Hamilton Palace Sale," *London Times*, July 10, 1882; Hamilton 2, p. 136, no. 1013 (as Rubens and Wildens, "Milking Time"); M. H. Arnot, no. 18; Permanent Collection (1936), no. 42; Morse, pp. 146 and 188; Faison, p. 189; Permanent Collection (1973), p. 89 (as Anonymous, "The Farm at Laeken").

ANONYMOUS

53 The Mill Pond
after Meindert Hobbema
Oil on canvas 24¹/₈ x 32³/₄ inches
n.s.

PROVENANCE: Hinman Barrett Hurlbut; Matthias H. Arnot, 1883 (Hurlbut collection sale); by bequest to the Arnot Art Gallery, 1910.

LITERATURE: M. H. Arnot, no. 42 (as by Hobbema); Permanent Collection (1936), no. 53 (as by Hobbema, attrib.); Morse, p. 188; Permanent Collection (1973), p. 109 (as by Hobbema).

SIMONE STONE (attrib.), Head of Charles II, When a Boy

ANONYMOUS, The Mill Pond

ANONYMOUS, The Farm at Laken (Milking Time)

CHARLES-FRANCOIS DAUBIGNY   French, 1817-1878

2 **On the Oise**, ca. 1861
Oil on canvas 15⅛ x 26½ inches
Stamped LR: VENTE DAUBIGNY

PROVENANCE: S. M. Vose, 1878 (artist's estate sale); Wynkoop collection (?) ; Matthias H. Arnot, by 1900; by bequest to the Arnot Art Gallery, 1910.

LITERATURE: M. H. Arnot, no. 60; Permanent Collection (1936), no. 2; Faison, p. 189; Permanent Collection (1973), p. 100, illus. p. 101.

    The son of a landscape artist, Edme Daubigny, Daubigny was himself a champion of painting landscapes directly from nature. In his youth, he decorated jewelry boxes and clockfaces; by 1834, he was working as a restorer in the Louvre and as a decorative painter at Versailles. In 1835, he began formal studies with Senties and later with Delaroche. He traveled to Italy in 1836 and throughout the 1840s he frequently visited the French countryside, regularly sumbitting landscapes to the Salons. He won a second class medal in 1848. In the 1850s, be befriended Corot and traveled with him to Switzerland and through the French countryside. His travels around France were aided by his purchase, in 1857, of *le Botin*, a small flat-bottomed boat with a cabin to serve as a floating studio. Every summer Daubigny would cruise the rivers of France to sketch out of doors. His paintings won him many admirers, followers and official honors, including first class medals in the Salons of 1853 and 1857, an appointment as Chevalier of the Legion of Honor in 1859, state commissions, and in the 1860s, selection as juror for the Salons.
    Daubigny was committed to *plein air* painting, producing spontaneous landscape studies directly from nature, as well as more finished studio pieces prepared for the Salons. In 1860, Daubigny purchased a plot of land at Auvers-sur-Oise where he built a cottage, known as the Villa des Vallées, to provide a winter mooring for *le Botin*. *On the Oise* most likely dates from this period. Painted entirely *en plein air* on the river Oise, this painting reveals Daubigny's sensitivity to light, both in the handling of the sky as the blue-grey tones fade to the pink-tinged horizon and in the treatment of the sky reflected in the water. Daubigny delighted in such casual incidents of nature as cows grazing beside the river and a man lounging on the grass.

PIERRE ETIENNE THEODORE ROUSSEAU   French, 1812-1867

3 **An Autumn Evening**, n.d.
Oil on panel 10⅞ x 15¹¹⁄₁₆ inches
Signed LR: TH. Rousseau

PROVENANCE: Marmontel collection, 1867 (Arts Club sale, Paris); Albert Spencer; Matthias H. Arnot, 1888 (Spencer collection sale); by bequest to the Arnot Art Gallery, 1910.

LITERATURE: M. H. Arnot, no. 51.; Permanent Collection (1936), no. 3. Faison, p. 189.; Permanent Collection (1973), p. 130, illus. p. 131.

    Rousseau, the guiding spirit of the Barbizon artists, developed an interest in landscape painting early in life when his mother's cousin introduced him to sketching in the forest of Compiègne. He briefly studied classical landscape painting with Rémond and Guillon-Lethière, as well as studying at the Louvre, in particular the works of Claude Lorrain (acc. no. 32) and the van de Veldes (acc. nos. 50 and 51). He submitted his first landscapes to the Salon of 1831 and won a third class medal in 1834. From 1836 to 1848, his works were regularly rejected from the Salons by jurors who criticized the lack of finish and Rousseau's "raw" portrayal of nature. Despite the absence of official support, Rousseau's reputation grew as his fresh approach to landscape painting gained the endorsement of such colleagues and critics as Delacroix, Théophile Gautier, and Théophile Thoré. In subsequent years, Rousseau's paintings received the official acclaim they deserved: he won first class medals in the Salon of 1849 and the Exposition Universelle of 1855 when thirteen of his paintings were shown, confirming his reputation as one of the principal landscapists of his age.
    Rousseau's lasting reputation was assured by the landscapes painted *en plein air* in Barbizon and the Forest of Fountainbleau. The Barbizon artists, primarily Rousseau, Millet (acc. no. 4), and Diaz de la Peña (acc. no. 1), found inspiration in this rural setting and painted the peasant, his world, and the surrounding landscape. Rousseau first visited the village of Barbizon in 1826, rented a studio there after 1837, and settled there permanently in 1846. *An Autumn Evening* is a rural scene in the environs of Barbizon. In the center of the painting, on the horizon, the dwindling light from the recent sundown barely illuminates the murky twilight of the forest. The freely painted landscape is built up with washes of brown paint. The more delicately painted evening sky has subtle gradations of creamy white and yellow highlights on the deeper grey clouds. The whole work is thinly painted, allowing the pinkish brown of the underpainting to add depth to the scene.
    Rousseau's financial insecurity forced him to organize sales of his paintings in the 1860s. *An Autumn Evening* was purchased for the Marmontel collection from the sale of over one hundred of the artist's works held at the Arts Club in Paris in 1867, six months before Rousseau's death.

CHARLES-FRANCOIS DAUBIGNY, On the Oise; color plate p. 18

PIERRE ETIENNE THEODORE ROUSSEAU, An Autumn Evening

CHARLES-EMILE JACQUE   French, 1813-1894

9 Barn Yard, n.d.
Oil on panel 22¹/₈ x 17³/₈ inches
Signed LL: Ch. Jacque

PROVENANCE: Albert Spencer (?); Matthias H. Arnot, 1879; by bequest to the Arnot Art Gallery, 1910.

LITERATURE: *Catalogue: Loan Exhibition* (Elmira, NY: n.p., 1879), p. 49, no. 103; "The Loan Exhibition," *Elmira Daily Advertiser*, May 31, 1879; M. H. Arnot, no. 19; Permanent Collection (1936), no. 9; Permanent Collection (1973), p. 110, illus.

Jacque was born in Paris and his early training was with a cartographer. He executed prints depicting military life during his years in the army, 1830-1836, and submitted two of them to the Salon of 1833. Following his service, he spent two years in London where he engraved illustrations for a publication of Shakespeare's works. After hs return to Paris, he continued to work as an illustrator and established his reputation as a realist in the medium of etching, winning a third class medal for graphic arts in the Salon of 1850. Jacque began painting in 1845, met Millet (acc. no. 4) in 1847 and two years later both artists moved to Barbizon. After 1854, Jacque divided his time between Barbizon and Paris. His interest in fowls led Jacque to practice animal husbandry and in 1852 he published a monograph of foreign and domestic poultry. Chickens, sheep, and pigs constitute the subject matter of the bulk of his paintings; his fame as an animal painter rivaled that of Troyon and Rosa Bonheur. Jacque first exhibited his paintings at the Salon of 1848. He won a third class medal in 1861, second class in 1864, and he was named Chevalier of the Legion of Honor in 1867.

In the 1840s, after Jacque moved to Barbizon, he began to produce small paintings of poultry. The setting of *Barn Yard* is from the darkened interior of a barn where three hens walk on the hay strewn floor toward the bright sunlight of the barn yard, visible through the open door. The brightness of the background areas as seen in the central portion of the painting contrasts sharply with the foreground and draws the viewer in the painting, not unlike the hens scurrying out the door toward the barnyard.

NARCISSE VIRGILE DIAZ DE LA PENA   French, 1808-1876

1 In the Pyrenées, 1874
Oil on panel 10¹/₁₆ x 15⁹/₁₆ inches
Signed and dated LL: N. Diaz. 74

PROVENANCE: George I. Seney, 1867; Matthias H. Arnot, 1891 (Seney collection sale); by bequest to the Arnot Art Gallery, 1910.

LITERATURE: Seney, pp. 44 and 276, no. 280; "The Seney Sale is Ended," *New York Times*, February 14, 1891; M. H. Arnot, no. 67; Permanent Collection (1936), no. 1; Faison, p. 189; Permanent Collection (1973), p. 102, illus. p. 103.

Diaz de la Peña was the son of Spanish exiles residing in Bordeaux. Between 1825 and 1830, he was already working in Paris as an apprentice decorator in a porcelain factory. Though he briefly studied drawing with François Souchon, a former pupil of J.-L. David, Diaz was essentially self-taught, copying works in the Louvre. He evolved a style that blended his taste for eighteenth-century rococo with more contemporary trends, such as Romanticism and Orientalism, the latter from his association with the painter A.G. Decamps. He exhibited works of mythological and religious subjects but became best known for landscapes after meeting Rousseau (acc. no. 3) in Barbizon in 1837. Every year, Diaz returned to the village of Barbizon in the Fountainbleau Forest to paint from nature, he also traveled to other regions of France, including the Alps, Etretat on the Normandy coast, and Honfleur. His sense of color and his physical handling and shaping of paint established his reputation. Unlike the rejections suffered by other Barbizon artists, Diaz's works regularly received official approval. He first exhibited in the Salon of 1831 and continued to successfully exhibit his works until 1859. He won a third class medal in 1844, second class in 1846, first class in 1848, and, in 1851, he was made a Chevalier of the Legion of Honor.

Diaz's success at the Salons is due in part to his approach to landscape painting. Rather than painting pure landscapes, Diaz painted *scènes galantes*, pastoral scenery peopled with gypsies, peasants, or nymphs. *In the Pyrenées*, painted late in his career, is one such picturesque scene. Two peasants walk with their sheep along a path in a marshy plain under a partially overcast sky. Light reflections dramatically set off the snow-covered mountains in the background and contrast sharply with the dense forest in the middle ground. The artist achieved the appearance of a tapestry by dabbling and scumbling ochres, golden yellows and tones of greens and bronzes over the field.

CHARLES-EMILE JACQUE, Barn Yard

NARCISSE VIRGILE DIAZ DE LA PENA, In the Pyrenées; color plate p. 19

CONSTANT TROYON   French, 1810-1865

7 The Red Cow, n.d.
Oil on canvas 37¼ x 29⅜ inches
Initialed LL: C. T.
Stamped LR: VENTE TROYON

PROVENANCE: George I. Seney, 1865 (?) (artist's estate sale?); Matthias H. Arnot, 1891 (Seney collection sale); by bequest to the Arnot Art Gallery, 1910.

LITERATURE: Seney, pp. 115 and 205, no. 147; "High Bids for Paintings," *New York Times*, February 13, 1891; M. H. Arnot, no. 63; I. Souville, *Constant Troyon: Les Grandes Peintures au ventes publiques* (1900), p. 43; Permanent Collection (1936), no. 7; Faison, p. 189; Permanent Collection (1973), p. 136, illus.

Troyon was born in Sèvres and was the third generation of his family to work in its celebrated porcelain factory. He never received formal training in painting but he did benefit from the advice of landscape painters Camille Roqueplan, whom he encountered in the forest of St. Cloud in 1831, and the Barbizon artist Theodore Rousseau (acc. no. 3). Troyon made his Salon début in 1833, with landscapes of the environs of his native region. His travels around the French countryside, including Barbizon and the Fountainbleau Forest, broadened his range of landscape studies. In 1841, he visited Normandy to paint with J. R. Brascassat, a specialist in farm animal subjects. The animal paintings of seventeenth-century Dutch artists Paulus Potter and Albert Cuyp, seen during his 1847 trip to Holland and Belgium, had enormous impact on the artist and, after his return to France, Troyon similarly devoted himself to portraying farm animals in landscapes. He won a third class medal in the Salon of 1838, second class in 1840, first class in the Salons of 1846, 1848 and 1855 and, in 1849, he was appointed Chevalier of the Legion of Honor. Throughout the 1850s, he worked in Normandy and met many of the other artists working there, including Bonvin and Jongkind, a precursor of Impressionism. He attracted a number of followers, in particular Emile van Marcke (acc. no. 8). After 1859, Troyon ceased to submit works to the Salon, perferring instead to participate in regional exhibitions in Bordeaux, Le Havre, Marseilles and Besançon, as well as foreign exhibitions in Brussels, Rotterdam and London. At his death, Troyon was named the premier animal painter of his era.

The Red Cow illustrates Troyon's devotion to and sensitivity for his preferred subject, farm animals. A lone cow dominates the landscape setting, as the bulkiness of the body looms over the horizon. The cow, pausing mid-step, looks out of the canvas, appearing as interested in the artist as the artist was in her. Troyon worked quickly, thinly painting the background landscape in order to concentrate on the animal before him.

CONSTANT TROYON, The Red Cow

EMILE VAN MARCKE   French, 1827-1890

8 Cattle in a Pool, n.d.
Oil on canvas 11 1/8 x 16 1/2 inches
Signed LL: Em van Marcke

PROVENANCE: Matthias H. Arnot, by 1879; by bequest to the Arnot Art Gallery, 1910.

LITERATURE: *Catalogue: Loan Exhibiton* (Elmira, NY: n.p., 1879), p. 49, no. 101; "The Loan Exhibition," *Elmira Daily Advertiser*, May 31, 1879; M. H. Arnot, no. 24; Permanent Collection (1936), no. 8, illus. p. 32; Permanent Collection (1973), p. 138.

Like his mentor Troyon (acc. no. 7), van Marcke was born in Sèvres, where his father, Jean-Baptiste, worked in the porcelain factory after studying painting with C. J. Watelet. In 1831, the family returned to Belgium and, in time, Emile was enrolled in the drawing classes at the local art academy in Liège. He later returned to France and, from 1853 to 1862, served as a decorator at the Sèvres factory where he met Troyon. The older artist encouraged van Marcke to work in oil and to paint landscapes directly from nature. To further his art, van Marcke attended agricultural schools and traveled to various regions of France to study animals and the landscape. His preferred subjects were the cattle of Normandy and eventually he bought a farmhouse at Bouttencourt. Van Marcke's Salon début was in 1857 and he won medals in the Salons of 1867, 1869 and 1870 before attaining a first class medal in 1878. In 1872, he was appointed Chevalier of the Legion of Honor. After Troyon's death in 1865, van Marcke was esteemed by many collectors to be the foremost cattle painter.

Typical of van Marcke's work is *Cattle in a Pool*. Two cows in the foreground stand in a pool of water, one nuzzling the other's neck while both look directly toward the artist, cautiously studying the intruder. In the background, several cows are in the field eating the grasses under a heavily overcast sky.

EMILE VAN MARKE, Cattle in a Pool

JEAN-FRANCOIS MILLET   French, 1814-1875

4 Apple Gatherers, 1851
Oil on canvas 15⁷/₁₆ x 12¹/₈ inches
Signed LR: J. F. Millet

PROVENANCE: Mary Jane Morgan; J. J. Hill, 1886 (Morgan collection sale); Knoedler & Co.; Marianna Arnot Ogden, 1893; by bequest to Matthias H. Arnot, 1904; by bequest to the Arnot Art Gallery, 1910.

LITERATURE: Morgan, pp. 24 and 49, no. 71 (as "Gathering Apples"); "The Morgan Collection," *New York Times*, March 1, 1886; "Buying Fine Paintings: Sale of Mrs. Morgan's Art Collection," *New York Times*, March 4, 1886; "The Morgan Pictures," *New York Herald*, March 5, 1886; C. H. Stranahan, *A History of French Painting* (NY: Charles Scribner's Sons, 1888), p. 375 (as "Gathering Apples"); Etienne Moreau-Nelaton, *Millet: Raconté par lui-même*, 3 vols. (Paris: Henry Laurens, 1921), 1:93, fig. 67; Permanent Collection (1936), no. 4; Morse, p. 188; Faison, p. 189.; Permanent Collection (1973), p. 122, illus.

Millet was from the small village of Gruchy near Cherbourg. His parents, though farmers, recognized and encouraged his interest in art. His early training was with local painters, Mauchel and Langois, both pupils of Baron Gros. In 1837, the city of Cherbourg awarded Millet a pension to study in Paris where he entered the studio of Delaroche. After failing to win medals, Millet withdrew and continued his education in the independant Académie Suisse and in the galleries of the Louvre. His Salon début was in 1840, when he submitted a portrait of a relative. After a decade of painting mythological subjects and nudes, Millet's interests turned to realism when he met Daumier and such Barbizon artists as Diaz, Rousseau, Jacque and Troyon (acc. nos. 1, 3, 9, and 7) in the late 1840s. Reflecting his heritage, Millet's perferred subject was the life of the French peasant; in 1848 he substituted a peasant subject, *Le Repos des faneurs (The Haymaker's Rest)* for a religious subject in his state commission. The proceeds of this sale permitted him and his family to move to Barbizon where he remained for the rest of his life. Though some critics were hostile to his work, Millet's peasant subjects, painted with the grandeur and nobility usually reserved for history paintings, brought him wide recognition and patronage. He won a second class medal in the Salons of 1853 and 1864 and a first class medal at the Exposition Universelle of 1867. The support of the American painter William Morris Hunt brought Millet's work to the attention and collections of may wealthy Americans, particularly in the Boston area. Millet's success with city dwellers has been explained by Robert Herbert as a denial of the pressures of modern life and nostalgia for simpler times:

> *Millet's world was one of labor and well-earned repose that permitted the urban bourgeoisie to release itself into the realm of the seemingly untouched past, with its connotations of permanence, health, open air, and simplicity of life.* (*Jean-François Millet*, London: Hayward Gallery, 1976, p. 14.)

Apple Gatherers is considered by Moreau-Nelaton as one of four allegories of the seasons painted for one of the artist's principal patrons, Alfred Feydeau. This painting of peasants harvesting apples is "Autumn." (Another painting in this series of allegories is the study for the *Gleaners*, or *Summer*, dated circa 1852-1853, and is reproduced in Gabriel P. Weisberg, *The Realist Tradition: French Painting and Drawing, 1830-1900*, Cleveland: Cleveland Museum of Art, 1980, p. 85, cat. no. 51, illus. p. 84.) Millet's focus on the anonymous peasants and their prosaic actions give a somber air to his portraits of the laborers of the land. Gathering apples is not lighthearted diversion; it is difficult, cramped work, done crouched over on hands and knees. This image does not glorify the bounty of nature or the nobility of working the soil. Rather it is a truthful representation of the hardships of labor. Such realistic portrayals suggested to some viewers Millet's political intention to expose the conditions of the rural peasants and their struggle to survive during the Second Empire (see T. J. Clarke, *The Absolute Bourgeois: Artists and Politics in France, 1848-1851*, Greenwich: New York Graphic Society, 1973, pp. 79-80.)

LUCIEN-ALPHONSE GROS   French, 1845-1913

11 Halt of Cavaliers, 1868-1869
Oil on canvas 22 x 18¹/₄ inches
Signed and dated LL: Lucien Gros 1868-69

PROVENANCE: Hinman Barrett Hurlbut; Matthias H. Arnot, 1883 (Hurlbut collection sale); by bequest to the Arnot Art Gallery, 1910.

LITERATURE: *Explication des ouvrages... exposés au Palais des Champs-Elysées* (Paris: Charles de Mourgues Freres, 1869), p. 150, no. 1111; M.H. Arnot, no. 36; Permanent Collection (1936), no. 11, illus. p. 22; Permanent Collection (1973), p. 108.

Gros was born in Wesserling. He studied with Meissonier (acc. nos. 14 and 15) and made his Salon début in 1865, winning medals in the Salons of 1867 and 1876. Meissonier's taste for historical genre was acquired by his student as is illustrated in this seventeenth-century genre scene. *Halt of Cavaliers*, two horsemen relaxing in the woods while their horses rest, was exhibited in the Salon of 1869. The historical theme for this work appears to be a pretext for the artist's obvious delight with and confidence in painting the sylvan retreat of sun-dappled trees and grasses.

JEAN-FRANCOIS MILLET, Apple Gatherers; color plate p. 16

LUCIEN-ALPHONSE GROS, Halt of Cavaliers

JEAN-LOUIS-ERNEST MEISSONIER   French, 1815-1891

14 Playing Bowles in the Fosse at Antibes, 1885
Oil on panel 17½ x 30¼ inches
Signed and dated LR: Meissonier 1885

PROVENANCE: George Emmanuel Secretan; George I. Seney, 1889 (Secretan collection sale); Matthias H. Arnot, 1891 (Seney collection sale); by bequest to the Arnot Art Gallery, 1910.

LITERATURE: Seney, pp. 87 and 226, no. 190. "High Bids for Paintings," *New York Times*, February 13, 1891; M. H. Arnot, no. 65; Permanent Collection (1936), no. 14; Faison, pp. 189-190, illus.; Permanent Collection (1973), p. 118, illus. p. 119; Hilton Kramer, "A Show to Celebrate America's Delight in French Art," *New York Times*, October 30, 1977.

Meissonier was perhaps the most eminent artist of his generation. His small, meticulously rendered genre paintings and military scenes won him many honors and in 1878, he was the first artist to be awarded the Grand Cross of the Legion of Honor.
Born in Lyons, Meissonier came to Paris as a child but returned to his native town to study classics and mathematics. He completed his education in Grenoble and then became an apprentice to a pharmacist. He began art studies after overcoming his father's objections and, in 1832, Meissonier entered the studio of A. J. Potier and later that of Leon Cogniet, where he met C. F. Daubigny (acc. no. 2) and Daumier. He began copying the Dutch and Flemish masters of the seventeenth century, particularly Terborch, Metzu and Dou, and the eighteenth-century French masters Greuze and Chardin. He continued pursuing his interest in *plein air* painting at the same time. His Salon début was in 1834 when he exhibited an historical genre subject, *A Visit to the Burgomaster*. In succeeding years, his small, finely detailed period subjects won him official recognition and a growing clientele. In the Salon of 1840, he won a third class medal, a second class the following year, and a first class medal in 1843. In 1855, Napoleon III purchased one of his genre scenes to give to Prince Albert as a memento of his visit to Paris. Meissonier was named Chevalier of the Legion of Honor in 1846, Officer of the Legion ten years later, and Commandeur of the Legion of Honor in 1867 when he was one of the featured French artists of the Exposition Universelle.
Like his approach to historical genre, Meissonier gave the same careful attention to the detail in his depiction of more contemporary events. In 1859, at the outbreak of the Austro-Italian War, Meissonier accompanied the French Army and recorded its exploits at Solferino. In subsequent years, he began a cycle of paintings based on the life of Napoleon I (only two were completed: the battlefield at Friedland, titled *1807*, now in the Metropolitan Museum of Art; and *1814*, illustrating the retreat from Moscow, in the Louvre).
Playing Bowles in the Fosse at Antibes depicts the artist and his friends and family relaxing out of doors and indulging in the French game of *boules* outside the walls of an old fortress in the south of France. The Arnot Art Museum owns an inscribed photograph of the painting identifying ten of the figures (see illustration at right). Meissonier is shown on the left, standing with his son and the painters Lucien-Alphonse Gros (acc. no. 11) and Edward Detaille. The American artist Daniel Ridgway Knight is one of the players in shirtsleeves in the center background and, at the right, Mme. Meissonier sits in the carriage. The artist's son Charles is again depicted standing beside her. In this painting, the artist combines his style of precise, highly-focused detail with the more broadly painted landscape, the smooth walls of the fortress shimmering in the sunlight and the foreground greenery an impressionistic massing of brushstrokes.

Note: There is no record of when or how the inscribed photograph of the painting entered the collection. Matthias Arnot may have acquired it when he purchased the painting from the 1891 Seney collection sale but neither the sale catalogue nor newspaper accounts include it.

JEAN-LOUIS-ERNEST MEISSONIER   French, 1815-1891

15 The Stirrup Cup, n.d.
Oil on panel 5 x 3½ inches
Signed LR: Meissonier

PROVENANCE: James H. Stebbins; Matthias H. Arnot, 1889 (Stebbins collection sale); by bequest to the Arnot Art Gallery, 1910.

LITERATURE: *The Art Treasures of America*, ed. Edward Strahan [Earl Shinn], 3 vols. (Philadelphia: George Barrie, 1880), 1:98 and 106; C. H. Stranahan, *A History of French Painting* (NY: Charles Scribner's Sons, 1888), p. 344; M. H. Arnot, no. 53; Permanent Collection (1936), no. 15, illus. p. 16 (as "The Inn Door"); *Public Art in Elmira, N.Y.* (Elmira: Association of Commerce, n.d.), illus. p. 34; Wesley Towner, *The Elegant Auctioneers* (NY: Hill and Wang, 1970), p. 122; Permanent Collection (1973), p. 118, illus.

For his historical subjects, Meissonier's preparation involved research and innumerable sketches to convincingly capture the ambience and flavor of the period. His remarkable technical skill and accuracy of detail is evident even in the smallest of his works. *The Stirrup Cup* is a genre scene of the seventeenth century, representing a man serving drink from a tray to another man on horseback in front of an inn. The figures and the horse are perfectly rendered: the costumes reveal the artist's intimate familiarity with the appearance and substance of period dress; the handling of the light and architectural detail of the setting give the work an immediacy and authority that belies its modest size. The theme of an innkeeper serving mounted riders was used by Meissonier in other paintings. This particular arrangement of figures is included in the larger *Halt at the Inn*, dated ca. 1865 and in the Wallace Collection, London. Wesley Towner, writing about the great auctions of the late nineteenth century, reproached the unidentified buyer of this "smaller than a penny post card" painting from the 1889 Stebbins sale who, for the $7,100 spent on the Meissonier, might have purchased instead two dozen Impressionist works.

1. E. Meissonier - The Artist's portrait
2. Chas Meissonier - Son of the Artist
3. Lucien Gros - Pupil of Meissonier
4. Ed Detaille - Artist
5. Bretegnier - Friend of the Artist
6. Maurice Courant - Marine painter
7. Pascal - Favorite Model of Meiss
8. Ridgway Knight - American Artist
9. Chas Meissonier - Again
10. Madame Meissonier - Wife of the Artist
    The Carriage - Horse and Dogs are all Meissonier's
11. Dr Rostan

JEAN-LOUIS-ERNEST MEISSONIER, Playing Bowles in the Fosse at Antibes; color plate p. 21

JEAN-LOUIS-ERNEST MEISSONIER, The Stirrup Cup; color plate p. 20

JULES-ADOLPHE BRETON   French, 1827-1906

6 Le Soir (Evening), 1880
Oil on canvas 48³/₄ x 78¹/₄ inches
Signed and dated LR: Jules Breton / Courrières 1880

PROVENANCE: Albert Spencer, 1880; Matthias H. Arnot, 1888 (Spencer collection sale); by bequest to Arnot Art Gallery, 1910.

LITERATURE: *Explication des ouvrages . . . exposés au Palais des Champs-Elysées* (Paris: Imprimerie Nationale, 1880), p. 49, no. 487; Charles M. Bigot, "Le Salon de 1880," *Revue politique et litteraire*, 2nd series, 18 (May 22, 1880):1109; Philippe de Chennevieres, "Le Salon de 1880," *Gazette des Beaux-Arts*, 2nd series, 21 (June 1880):505-506; Maurice du Seigneur, *L'Art et les artistes au Salon de 1880* (Paris: 1880); A. Hustin, "Jules Breton," *L'Estafette*, September 9, 1880; Paul Mantz, "Le Salon," *Le Temps*, May 9, 1880; Emile Michel, "Le Salon de 1880," *Revue des deux mondes*, 3rd series, 39 (June 1, 1880):692; *The Art Treasures of America*, ed. Edward Strahan [Earl Shinn], 3 vols. (Philadelphia: George Barrie, 1880), 3:123; Paul Lefort, "L'Exposition Nationale de 1883: La Peinture," *Gazette des Beaux-Arts*, 2nd series, 28 (November 1883):385-386; C. H. Stranahan, *A History of French Painting* (NY: Charles Scribner's Sons, 1888), p. 386; M. H. Arnot, no. 52; Marius Vachon, *Jules Breton* (Paris: A. Lahure, 1899), p. 88; Permanent Collection (1936), no. 6, illus. p. 14; *Public Art in Elmira, N.Y.* (Elmira: Association of Commerce, n.d.), illus. p. 33; Faison, p. 190; Permanent Collection (1973), p. 93, illus. p. 94; Hollister Sturges, *Jules Breton and the French Rural Tradition* (Omaha, NE: Joslyn Art Museum and NY: The Arts Publisher, Inc., 1982), pp. 20, 96-97, no. 41, illus. p. 97; *A Pastoral Legacy: Paintings and Drawings by the American Artists Ridgway Knight and Aston Knight* (Ithaca: Herbert F. Johnson Museum of Art, 1989), [p. 9], fig. 4.

Breton, France's premier painter of peasant life, was born to a prosperous peasant family in the rural community of Courrières. His early schooling was in a local Catholic seminary; he later received a classical education at the college of Douai where he took his first drawing course under Father Wallet. He continued his art training in Belgium and, from 1847 on, in Paris at the atelier of M.-M. Drolling. He maintained a studio in his native town of Courrières so he could observe the traditions, rituals, and festival of rural life. Breton's early submissions to the Salons of 1849 and 1851 were realistic portrayals of the hardships of the laboring classes. Breton soon turned away from social realism to create large scenes of peasant life showing a more idealized naturalism; he won a third class medal in the Salon of 1855 for *The Gleaners*. Renowned for his sentimental and romantic portrayals of rural life, Breton was critized for his lack of realism in portraying the often ugly conditions of France's poorer classes. Unlike Millet (acc. no. 4) who emphatized with the laborer's pain and fatigue, Breton's approach allowed him to celebrate peasant life by lending grandeur to the common man and poetry to his simple values. Breton's romantic vision of peasant life proved quite popular and official approval was not lacking; he won a second class medal in 1857, first class in 1859, 1861 and 1867, appointed Chevalier of the Legion of Honor in 1861, Officer of the Legion of Honor in 1867, Commandeur of the Legion of Honor in 1872, and in 1866, he was elected to the Institut de France. Breton's successes established his international reputation. Wealthy American collectors were especially attracted to Breton's purity, his reverance for nature, his noble models, and the correct moral emphasis of his paintings.

Le Soir was Breton's celebrated entry to the Salon of 1880 and the painting referred to by S. P. Avery in his June 17-19 diary entries of a "sale of Breton to Spencer" (*The Diaries, 1871-1882, of Samuel P. Avery, Art Dealer*, ed. by M. F. Beaufort, H. L. Kleinfield, and J. K. Welcher, NY: Arno Press, 1977, pp. 575-576. Avery's April 24 entry notes that he bought Breton's Salon painting from Goupil for 40.000 francs. See p. 547.) In this painting, Breton depicts a group of women weeding in the left background but gives greater prominence to the three beautiful and surprisingly clean women resting in the right foreground, in particular, the woman standing and adjusting her jacket. The delicately hued twilight sky and the vibrant setting sun casts an air of melancholy over the darkening plain, a sentiment that, as Sturges points out, is hardly warranted in the subject of weeders at the end of their working day. This element of sadness was enhanced by Breton's inclusion of a few lines from his newly-published poem Jeanne to the Salon catalogue entry, thereby complicating the meaning of both. In his selected passage, Breton celebrated weeders working the fields until the evening, the setting sun's "sublime fire" magnifying the glory of their work.

> *Sarcleuses, qui trainez encor vos genoux lents*
> *Sur les blés, où le soir met des joyaux tremblants;*
> *Qui retenez l'azur dans vos plis; l'astre énorme*
> *D'un trait de feu sublime agrandit votre forme;*
> *Sur vos fronts, dans sa gloire, il rayonne vermeil.*
> *Filles, prosternez-vous, adorez le soleil!*

Breton's reputation as a poet-painter was established with the publication in 1875 of his collection of poems *Les Champs et la mer* and in 1880 with the single long poem of *Jeanne*. Breton's twin talents appealed to American collectors who often accompanied the listings of his paintings in their collection catalogues with related poems. Matthias Arnot included a translated passage of a Breton poem in his catalogue to underscore the freedom evening brings to toilers of the soil:

> "Still lingering"
> *Below the flaming prisms of the sunset glow,*
> *Outflowing from infinity, the pure celestial atoms*
> *Float in iridescence through the aroma ladened air.*
> *The azure blue still trembles ineffable and pale;*
> *Tis the hour of exquisite delight, when, forgetting*
> *The snares of the world and its bitter pains,*
> *The soul freely opens its wings to aimless fancy.*

JULES-ADOLPHE BRETON, Le Soir; color plate p. 6

JEAN-LEON GEROME   French, 1824-1904

12 The Marabou (At the Door of His House), 1889
Oil on canvas 29 x 23¹/₂ inches
Signed LR: J. L. GEROME

PROVENANCE: Wynkoop collection (?); Matthias H. Arnot, by 1900; by bequest to the Arnot Art Gallery, 1910.

LITERATURE: F. F. Herring, *The Life and Works of Jean-Léon Gérôme* (NY: Cassell, 1892), p. 200; M. H. Arnot, no. 57; Permanent Collection (1936), no. 12; Faison, p. 190, illus.; Permanent Collection (1973), p. 105, illus. p. 106; Gerald M. Ackerman, *The Life and Work of Jean-Léon Gérôme* (NY: Sotheby's Publications, 1986), p. 264, no. 371, illus. p. 265.

    Gérôme, leader of the "Néo-Grec" School of painting and an influential teacher at the Ecole des Beaux-Arts, was one of the most successful artists of the nineteenth century. In his works of historical subjects and contemporary foreign genre scenes, his commitment to verisimilitude resulted in a style now termed Objective Realism.
    The son of a silversmith, Gérôme studied drawing at the school in his native town of Vésoul before entering the Paris atelier of Delaroche in 1840. A prize student, he accompanied his master to Rome in 1844 and, on his return to Paris the following year, he studied briefly with Gleyre, who had taken over Delaroche's atelier. He competed unsuccessfully for the Prix de Rome in 1846, but with Delaroche's encouragement he entered a large classical genre subject in the Salon of 1847. This painting, *Combat de Coqs*, won a third class medal and was singled out for praise by the influential critic Théophile Gautier. Gérôme's success attracted a number of Gérôme's fellow students from Gleyre's studio to emulate his style. This group of artists, with Gérôme as their leader, was termed the *Néo-Grecques* or *Pompeistes* in recognition of their source of inspiration, Greek vase painting and Roman wall murals. Gérôme's Salon success also led to several lucrative state commissions, including wall panels for Prince Napoleon's Pompeian palace. In 1856, Gérôme traveled to Egypt with four friends spending eight months on a Nile houseboat and in Cairo. This and subsequent trips to the Near East, to Constantinople and Asia Minor through the mid-1870s resulted in entirely new subjects for the artist. His meticulously detailed genre paintings of classical history, costume pieces and Orientalist scenes were enormously popular and brought Gérôme great honor and notoriety. He won second class medals in the Salons of 1848 and 1855, was appointed Chevalier of the Legion of Honor in 1855, an Officer of the Legion in 1867 and Commandeur in 1878. In 1865, he was made a member of the Institut de France. Gérôme took up the medium of sculpture in 1878, winning a second class medal that year and a first class medal in 1881. In 1863 he became a professor at the Ecole des Beaux-Arts, a post he held until 1902. His teachings and influence touched a long succession of French and American students and his home became a popular gathering place for friends and admirers, including Baudry, Cabanal, George Sand and Gautier. Gérôme is also noted for his vigorous campaign against the Impressionists, in particular Manet, though Gérôme remained a lifelong friend of Degas.
    The Marabou (At the Door of His House) is a Cairo scene of an elegant Arab leaning against a door jamb while a marabou, a species of stork, walks in the street in front of the door. (Ackerman maintains the marabou is a pet as the man is holding a whip.) The careful depiction of textures—the rough-hewn masonry with finely-carved decorations, the wood-grain of the door, the rich shimmer of the yellow satin robe, and the bird's soft plumage—is ample proof of Gérôme's attentive observation and artistic skills. The "ordinariness" of the genre scene, its appeal as a "document" of a Cairo street scene, and the lack of a complicated or a manufactured theme supports the artist's attempt at objective truth and implies he witnessed this scene, thereby giving the painting an almost hypnotic sense of reality.

JEAN-LEON GEROME   French, 1824-1904

13 The Rose (The Love Token), 1887
Oil on canvas 36¹/₂ x 24¹/₄ inches
Signed LL: J. L. GEROME

PROVENANCE: Boussod, Valadon, and Cie., Paris, 1887; Knoedler and Co., 1887; Matthias H. Arnot, by 1900; by bequest to the Arnot Art Gallery, 1910.

LITERATURE: M. H. Arnot, no. 49; *St. Louis* (Missouri) *Front Rank*, November 3, 1935, illus.; Permanent Collection (1936), no. 13, illus. p. 30; *Public Art in Elmira, N.Y.* (Elmira: Association of Commerce, n.d.), illus. p. 35; Permanent Collection (1973), p. 105, illus.; Gerald M. Ackerman, *The Life and Work of Jean-Léon Gérôme* (NY: Sotheby's Publications, 1986), pp. 132 and 260, no. 351, illus. p. 261.

    Like *The Marabou* (acc. no. 12), *The Rose* illustrates the artist's attention to minute details, including the carved inscription at the upper right proclaiming Mohammed the prophet of God, in order to convince the viewer that this, or something close to it, was witnessed by the artist. Yet the decidedly romantic overtones of the painting of a veiled woman on the balcony tossing a rose to an Arab on horseback below is, as Ackerman noted, "unexpected . . . for the usually stoic master" (p. 132). Gérôme was never known for emotional or sentimental subjects, perferring to capture his audience and his admirers with his objective recording of reality, assuring its veracity through the artist's travels or exhaustive research. However, according to Ackerman, in the late 1880s, Gérôme may have been inspired or encouraged by the Symbolist movement to heighten the emotional content of his genre scenes with implied literary themes. *The Rose* may be a variation of Romeo and Juliet, of proclaimed but frustrated love.
    Gérôme was the son-in-law of the Parisian art dealer and editor Adolphe Goupil, who also held reproduction rights to Gérôme's work and published fine photogravures. After Adolphe's death in 1884, his partner (and Gérôme's son-in-law) Etienne Valadon renamed the business Boussod, Valadon and Cie. and continued to carry Gérôme's work. Boussod, Valadon and Cie. sent this painting to their New York branch, Knoedler and Company.

JEAN-LEON GEROME, The Marabou
(At the Door of His House); color plate p. 3

JEAN-LEON GEROME, The Rose (The Love Token)

FREDERICK HENDRIK KAEMMERER   French, b. Netherlands, 1839-1892

21 Winter, n.d.
Oil on canvas 15¾ x 8¾ inches
Signed LL: F. H. KAEMMER.

PROVENANCE: Matthias H. Arnot, by 1900; by bequest to the Arnot Art Gallery, 1910.

LITERATURE: M. H. Arnot, no. 13; Permanent Collection (1936), no. 21; Permanent Collection (1973), p. 110, illus. p. 111.

    F.H. Kaemmerer was born in The Hague and after beginning his art training in his native town, moved to Paris and entered the atelier of Gérôme (acc. nos. 12 and 13). Kaemmerer was known for his small, exquisitely finished tableaux featuring society subjects of the Empire and the Directory. His anecdotal society painting *Wedding under the Directory* was well-received by the public and was followed by *A Baptism under the Directory* in the Salon of 1878. He achieved modest acclaim at the Salons, winning a medal in 1874. In 1889, he won a silver medal and an appointment as Chevalier of the Legion of Honor.

    His melancholic *Winter* depicts an upper class woman dressed in a fur-trimmed coat and veiled hat. She pauses before a bridge, apparently lost in her thoughts, sad and reflective. Figures skate on the ice in the backgound. The restricted palette (primarily black, white, and tones of grey and brown), is enlivened with the use of bright red for her stockings and the flower on her hat as well as in the delicate pink used on the ice beside the bridge and in the sky at upper left.

FREDERICK HENDRIK KAEMMERER, Winter

CHARLES BARGUE   French, 1825-1883

18 At His Devotions, n.d.
Oil on panel 19³/₄ x 11⁷/₈ inches
n.s.
PROVENANCE: Matthias H. Arnot, after 1900 (?); by bequest to the Arnot Art Gallery, 1910.
LITERATURE: Permanent Collection (1936), no. 18; Permanent Collection (1973), p. 90.

Bargue was a painter of Orientalist genre scenes. There is a little known about him and his exact relationship to Gérôme (acc. nos/ 12 and 13) is unclear. (Some scholars list Bargue as Gérôme's student but Ackerman, Gérôme's biographer, disagrees. See Gerald Ackerman, *The Life and Work of Jean-Léon Gérôme*, NY: Sotheby's Publications, 1986, p. 170.) He was born in Paris, suffered ill-health, and supported himself by making lithographs, winning medals in this area in the Salons of 1867 and 1868. Bargue's drawing skill and his meticulous attention to detail led to his collaboration with Gérôme in the late 1860s on a three-volume academic drawing course. This series (Charles Bargue, *Cours de Dessin, exécuté avec le concours de Gérôme*, 3 vols., Paris: Goupil & Cie., 1868-1870) methodically led the student from drawing after plaster casts, to copying drawings by Old Masters, and finally to charcoal exercises in preparation for drawing a live model. Bargue supplied the lithographs to be copied by the students and apparently the course was quite popular as finding a complete set of the volumes is rare and most of the plates are damaged from use. (Ackerman, p. 170, notes van Gogh worked through the course twice.)

Bargue's paintings were of Near Eastern themes and usually featured richly costumed figures in meticulously detailed settings. *At His Devotions* is a grisaille panel and illustrates a robed man kneeling on a carpet intently reading the book, most likely the Koran, placed on a stand in front of him. The intricately carved stairway and walls, the perforated metal lamp, and the patterning of the carpet all combine to give the appropriate exotic ambience. The restricted palette of this painting and the shorthand treatment of the details (note, for example, the incised lines in the lamp from the artist's use of the rounded end of his paintbrush handle) suggests it was a study for another painting or perhaps a model for a lithograph.

CHARLES BARGUE, At His Devotions

AUGUSTE BONHEUR   French, 1824-1884

31 Morning in the Highlands, n.d.
Oil on canvas 28³/₄ x 39¹/₂ inches
Signed LR: Auguste Bonheur

PROVENANCE: George I. Seney ; Matthias H. Arnot, 1891 (Seney Collection sale); by bequest to the Arnot Art Gallery, 1910.

LITERATURE: Seney, pp. 12 and 217, no. 171; "High Bids for Paintings," *New York Times*, February 13, 1891; M. H. Arnot, no. 64. Permanent Collection (1936), no. 31, illus. p. 20; Permanent Collection (1973), p. 91, illus. 92.

Bonheur came from a family of artists who specialized in animal subjects. Born in Bordeaux, Auguste's sisters were Rosa, who became one of the most celebrated animal painters of France, and Juliette, who also achieved fame as an animal painter; their brother was Isidore, the animal sculptor. All received initial training under their father, Raymond, a landscape painter. Like Rosa, Auguste specialized in landscapes with animals and occasionally assisted his sister in her commissions. (Mme. Micas Klumpke, Rosa's biographer and companion, kept a register of the artist's works and noted Auguste's payment for his assistance on a replica of Rosa's *Le Laborage nivernais: le Sombrage*. See Eric Zafran, *French Salon Paintings from Southern Collections*, Atlanta: The High Museum of Art, 1982, p. 51.) Though his fame was eclipsed by Rosa's international reputation, Auguste's paintings were greatly admired. He won a third class medal in the Salons of 1852 and 1857, a second class in 1859, and first class in 1861 and 1863. He was appointed Chevalier of the Legion of Honor in 1867. His paintings also found a receptive audience in Britain and he exhibited at the Royal Academy in London between 1857 and 1874.

Auguste's animal paintings are without the grandeur of treatment or the overriding theme of the harmonious union of man and nature that elevated Rosa's paintings to the top of the *animalier* genre. Auguste's works are of a quieter sort, revealing his sensitive observation of nature. Gautier remarked that Auguste's paintings were unexpectedly refreshing and, indeed, more faithful to nature for their lack of pretension and absence of painterly tricks:

> *Auguste Bonheur has dared—and it is great audacity—to unvarnish nature, to take away the smoke and the dirt, to wash off the bitumen sauce with which art ordinarily covers it, and he has painted it as he sees it.* (Théophile Gautier, *Abécédaire du Salon de 1861*, reproduced in Louis Viardot, *The Masterpieces of French Art*, 2 vols, Philadephia: Gebbie & Co., 1884, 1:80).

Morning in the Highlands depicts a group of sheep amid the quiet, pristine beauty of a mountainous landscape with early morning fog obscuring the distant hills. Auguste captures the natural behavior of the sheep who are still gathered in a close group from the previous night's rest and are just beginning to stir. His sensitive observation of light is matched by his skillful handling of paint in the modeling of the animals' fur.

AUGUSTE BONHEUR, Morning in the Highlands

GUSTAVE COURBET   French, 1819-1877

5 A Mountain Stream, ca. 1860
Oil on canvas 18¼ x 21¾ inches
Signed LR: G. Courbet

PROVENANCE: Wynkoop collection (?) ; Matthias H. Arnot, by 1900; by bequest to the Arnot Art Gallery, 1910.

LITERATURE: M. H. Arnot, no. 59; Permanent Collection (1936), no. 5; Morse, pp. 45 and 188; Faison, p. 189.

Courbet was born in Ornans, a small town in the region of eastern France called the Franche-Comté. His parents were prosperous landowners and encouraged their son's artistic leaning by enrolling him in a local seminary where he was taught to draw from nature by Father Beau, a former pupil of Baron Gros. Courbet later entered the Collège Royal in Besançon where he took additional drawing courses. In 1839, Courbet went to Paris, where he studied at the independant Académie Suisse, copied Old Masters in the Louvre, and was advised by Baron Charles Steuben and N. A. Hesse. He began submitting works to the Salons in 1841 but it was not until 1844 that one, a self-portrait, was accepted. His first award, a second class medal, was in 1849; he won other medals in 1857 and 1861.

In 1850, Courbet exhibited *The Burial of Ornans*, a provincial funeral presented with the grandeur and scale of a history painting. The audacity of this painting set off a critical storm and is now regarded as a pivotal work in the development of Realism. Like the Barbizon artists, Courbet preferred the landscapes of France and the daily lives of ordinary people as the subjects for his paintings. His mundane subjects were too unworthy and his unidealized portrayals of common people too "ugly" to be considered art. Courbet ignored his critics and when two of his works were rejected from the 1855 Exposition Universelle, he opened his own exhibition in a pavillion facing the Palais de l'Exposition under a banner titled "DU REALISME." He accompanied his works with a brochure that serves as a maifesto for Realism. Courbet's significance, according to Sarah Faunce, is his "authenticity" in that he was "asserting the claim that the experience of the individual self in the world is the only valid source of art" (Sarah Faunce and Linda Nochlin, *Courbet Reconsidered*, NY: The Brooklyn Museum, 1988, p. 7). Courbet's commitment to an art of his own time and of his own people was revolutionary when artists were being trained to paint themes of religious history, classical legend, or political heroism. His brash self-assurance and his contempt for official approval and the art establishment is evident in his refusal of the 1870 nomination to be Chevalier of the Legion of Honor.

A Mountain Stream features the chalky cliffs surrounding Ornans, elements in the landscape of his native region. Since his youth, he had sketched the grottos and geological formations of the Franche-Comté and as a mature artist he frequently painted the gorges and streams of the regions. This work most likely dates from the 1860s when Courbet increasingly relied upon the palette knife to suggest the physical substance of rocks and boulders. The work reflects the immediacy of Courbet's firsthand experience sketching on site as the artist shifted from a loaded brush to a palette knife. The rich surface texture enhances the play of light and shadow across the canvas.

PIERRE MARIE BEYLE   French, 1838-1902

30 Fishing for Sole, ca. 1881
Oil on canvas 39⅝ x 28 inches
Signed LL: Beyle

PROVENANCE: Mary Jane Morgan; Marianna Arnot Ogden, 1886 (Morgan collection sale); Matthias H. Arnot, by 1900; by bequest to the Arnot Art Gallery, 1910.

LITERATURE: Morgan, pp. 3 and 36, no. 4; "Buying Fine Paintings," *New York Times*, March 4, 1886; "The Morgan Pictures," *New York Herald*, March 5, 1886; M. H. Arnot, no. 39; Permanent Collection (1936), no. 30; Permanent Collection (1973), p. 91.

Born in Lyons, Beyle moved to Paris and made his Salon début in 1867. Between 1865 and 1870, several of his caricatures were published in Parisian journals. In the 1870s, he became known for his paintings of foreign subjects, in particular, those works inspired by his trip to Algeria in 1877-1878. Around 1881, he traveled to the Normandy coast where his marine landscapes and fishing scenes would later bring him honors at the Paris Salons, including a third class medal in 1881 and a second class medal in 1887.

Typical of Beyle's work are grandiose paintings of rather prosaic subjects. *Fishing for Sole* dates to the artist's Normandy period and depicts two peasant girls absorbed in the fishing line one of the girls is pulling out of the water. The finished treatment and contrived studio poses of the two girls is in sharp contrast with Beyle's less studied and more painterly treatment of the landscape and sea.

GUSTAVE COURBET, A Mountain Stream; color plate p. 17

PIERRE MARIE BEYLE, Fishing for Sole

MAURICE LELOIR   French, 1853-1940

25 Market Morning, 1880
Oil on panel 16⅝ x 23½ inches
Signed and dated LL: Maurice Leloir 1880

PROVENANCE: Wynkoop collection (?); Matthias H. Arnot, by 1900; by bequest to the Arnot Art Gallery, 1910.

LITERATURE: M. H. Arnot, no. 55; Permanent Collection (1936), no. 25; Permanent Collection (1973), p. 114.

   Leloir had wide-ranging interests and found success as a genre and history painter, an illustrator of literature, and a set designer for theatre and movies. He was born in Paris to a family of artists and studied with his father, Jean-Baptiste Auguste, his mother, Héloise Colin-Leloir, as well as her father, Alexandre Colin. He was a member and one-time president of the Société des aquarellistes français and he was an illustrator for the published works of Rousseau, Molière, and Balzac, among others. He designed stage sets for Sarah Bernhardt and later worked in Hollywood. In 1906, Leloir founded the Société de l'histoire du costume, serving as president until his death and assembling a noteworthy collection of sixteenth- to twentieth-century costumes which he bequeathed to the city of Paris and are the base collection for the city's Musée Municipal du Costume.
   Leloir's obsession with the decorative surface of people and objects perhaps distracted him from delving any deeper and his paintings are populated with genial, hardworking peasants in carefully organized, studio-generated landscapes. *Market Morning* depicts an elderly couple laden with baskets, accompanied by their goats and dog, making their way to town, visible in the center background. Other peasants walk on the road in front of them. The tidy landscape of pruned bushes and tended vines and trees reflect the peasants' industriousness; the faint rainbow at upper left promises their continued good fortune.

JULES-EMILE SAINTIN   French, 1829-1894

10 Two Oracles, 1872
Oil on canvas 29¾ x 19¼ inches
Signed and dated LR: Jules Emile Saintin / 1872

PROVENANCE: James H. Stebbins, 1872; by purchase to Matthias H. Arnot, 1889; by bequest to the Arnot Art Gallery, 1910.

LITERATURE: *Explication des ouvrages . . . exposés au Palais des Champs-Elysées* (Paris: Imprimerie Nationale, 1872), p. 207, no. 1365; *The Art Treasures of America*, ed. Edward Strahan [Earl Shinn], 3 vols. (Philadelphia: George Barrie, 1880), 1:103 and 106, illus. p. 104; Clarence Cook, *Art and Artists of Our Time*, 3 vols. (NY: Selmar Hess, 1888), 1:81; M.H. Arnot, no. 54; Permanent Collection (1936), no. 10; Permanent Collection (1973), p. 131, illus.

   Saintin was born in Lemé and studied under M.-M. Drolling, F. E. Picot and A. J. B. Leboucher. He quickly acquired a reputation in Paris for portraits and genre painting, winning medals in 1866 and 1870 and he was made Chevalier of the Legion of Honor in 1877. In 1862 he briefly visited New York City, where he received several portrait commissions.
   In 1861, Gérôme (acc. nos. 12 and 13) exhibited a painting entitled *Deux Augures (Two Oracles)* of two Roman priests, one laughing at the other's comment regarding the ancient proverb "two augurs can never encounter each other without laughing." The implication was that the pronouncements of oracles, taken seriously by their listeners, were easily ridiculed when two oracles were alone. Saintin's *Two Oracles* was exhibited in the Salon of 1872 under the title *Deux Augures* from the collection of "J. H. Steblins", a misspelling of the work's first owner, James H. Stebbins. Saintin presents this theme in modern terms: a pretty waiting maid admiring her employer's collection of Oriental objects, in particular the costumed Japanese warrior with an unsheathed knife. Saintin's *japonisme* was just one of many artworks inspired by the display of Japanese art at the 1867 Exposition Universelle, an event which created a rage for all things Japanese and which affected a diverse assortment of Salon painters as well as the more avant garde artists. Saintin was clearly less concerned with commenting on modern soothsayers than he was in capturing the rich textures and ornamental details of such *objets d'art*. The maid is presented with the same surface hardness and textural precision as the enameled objects beside her. As Cook noted about this particular painting, the artist "showed no little skill in the superficial imitation of stuffs and materials, in the lacquer of the Japanese figure for example, but he rarely gets below the surface."

MAURICE LELOIR, Market Morning

JULES-EMILE SAINTIN, Two Oracles; color plate p. 24

JEAN-JOSEPH BENJAMIN-CONSTANT   French, 1845-1902

19 Messaline, 1879
Oil on canvas 22 x 14^{11}/$_{16}$ inches
Signed and dated LR: Benjamin Constant.79
Inscribed verso UC: "Messaline" / B.C.

PROVENANCE: Albert Spencer; Matthias H. Arnot, 1888 (Spencer collection sale); by bequest to the Arnot Art Gallery, 1910.

LITERATURE: M. H. Arnot, no. 16; Permanent Collection (1936), no. 19; Permanent Collection (1973), p. 91.

Benjamin-Constant was born in Paris but entered the Ecole des Beaux-Arts in Toulouse and finished his studies at the école in Paris, studying in Cabanal's studio. He made his Salon début in 1869 with a painting based on a literary theme, *Hamlet and the King*, later purchased by the state. In 1870, during the Franco-Prussian War, he traveled through Spain, where he met the artist Mariano Fortuny. In 1872, he visited North Africa in the company of Charles Joseph Tissot, the ambassador to the Sultan in Morocco, and returned to France the following year with a vast collection of Islamic artifacts. Benjamin-Constant became a leading Orientalist painter in the 1870s and his work won a third class medal in the Salons of 1875 and 1878, a second class medal in 1876, and he was appointed Commandeur of the Legion of Honor in 1884. In the 1880s, Benjamin-Constant achieved considerable success as a society portraitist. In 1889 and again in 1893 he traveled to America where he established a reputation for portraiture and subsequently acquired an international clientele, including the future Edward VII, Queen Victoria, and Pope Leo XIII.

In his genre paintings, Benjamin-Constant specialized in mildly erotic harem scenes and history paintings with similarly engaging subjects. *Messaline* depicts the infamous Roman empress amid the splendor of the late Roman Empire. Messalina's sexual indiscretions were notorious and the subject of Juvenal's *Satires* (6-10). In 39 or 40 A.D., at age fourteen, Messalina became the third wife of her forty-eight year old second cousin, Claudius, who soon afterward ascended the imperial throne. During a temporary absence of her husband in 48 A.D., she openly celebrated a marriage to her favorite Silius and upon Claudius' return, he was compelled to put his wife and her lover to death. Benjamin-Constant presents the seductive Messalina, provacatively dressed, standing hand on hip, looking imperiously down on her audience, and waiting for action. This story of betrayal and retribution is presented with an antiquarian's eye for proper decor: the wall murals are decorated in the spare elegance of the so-called third style of Roman painting, fashionable in the first half of the first century A.D., and in the right background is a precise rendering of a Doric stoa. Messalina is surrounded by the sensuous clutter of a bedroom; note especially the leopard skin rug and Persian covers draped on the bed.

MARIE-FRANCOIS-FIRMIN GIRARD (FIRMIN-GIRARD)   French, 1838-1921

34 A Rainy Day, 1869
Oil on canvas 27^1/$_8$ x 51^3/$_8$ inches
Signed and dated LR: FIRMIN GIRARD 1869

PROVENANCE: Matthias H. Arnot, by 1900; by bequest to the Arnot Art Gallery, 1910.

LITERATURE: *Explication des ouvrages... exposés au Palais des Champs-Elysées* (Paris: Charles de Mourgues Freres, 1869), p. 141, no. 1046 (as "Surpris par l'orage"); M. H. Arnot, no. 17; Permanent Collection (1936), no. 34; Permanent Collection (1973), p. 107.

Firmin-Girard was born in Poncin and came to Paris in the mid-1850s where he entered Gleyre's studio. Initially, he preferred subjects of historical and religious themes and his 1859 Salon début was a painting of St. Sebastian. Firmin-Girard soon changed direction and began producing genre paintings which had more lucrative potential in the French art market. His highly finished, realistic paintings of everyday life were quite successful and he won a third class medal at the Salon of 1863 and a second class medal in 1872.

A Rainy Day was exhibited in the Salon of 1869 and depicts a family walking in the country and caught by surprise in the sudden outbreak of rain. Characteristic of Firmin-Girard was his microscopic attention to the smallest detail, from the sheen of satiny fabrics to the subtle variation in grey tones of the heavy clouds overhead, including the artist's signature rendered with its reflection in the storm puddle underneath. The highly finished and rather grandiose treatment of such a trivial event led C. H. Stranahan to remark that the artist "has power in giving elegance and brilliancy to inconsiderable subjects" (*A History of French Painting*, NY: Charles Scribner's Sons, 1888, p. 360).

JEAN-JOSEPH BENJAMIN-CONSTANT, Messaline; color plate p. 23

MARIE-FRANCOIS-FIRMIN GIRARD, A Rainy Day

JEHAN-GEORGES VIBERT   French, 1840-1902

20 The Cardinal's Menu, n.d.
Oil on panel 23½ x 28⅞ inches
Signed LL: J. G. Vibert

PROVENANCE: Mary Jane Morgan; Marianna Arnot Ogden, 1886 (Morgan collection sale); Matthias H. Arnot, by 1900; by bequest to the Arnot Art Gallery, 1910.

LITERATURE: Morgan, pp. 31 and 66, no. 153; "Mrs. Morgan's Paintings," *New York Times*, March 5, 1886; "The Morgan Pictures," *New York Herald*, March 5, 1886; "Mr. Arnot's Painting," *Elmira Daily Advertiser*, March 5, 1886; "The Art Sale Finished," *New York Times*, March 6, 1886; "Thousand's for Pictures," *Elmira Daily Advertiser*, March 6, 1886; C. H. Stranahan, *A History of French Painting* (NY: Charles Scribner's Sons, 1888), p. 348; Clarence Cook, *Art and Artists of Our Time*, 3 vols. (NY: Selmar Hess, 1888), 1:194; M. H. Arnot, no. 47; Permanent Collection (1936), no. 20, illus. p. 24; Permanent Collection (1973), p. 139, illus.

  Vibert was a master of satirical realism and his most frequent target was the clergy. Vibert was born in Paris and received his early training with his grandfather, the engraver J.-P.-M. Jazet. In 1856, he entered the Ecole des Beaux-Arts where he studied for six years, first under Barrias and later with Picot. His Salon début was in 1863 when he received an honorable mention for two genre subjects. For the next few years he painted large mythological subjects but his genre scenes of contemporary life received the highest praises. Vibert increasingly concentrated on small-scale and amusing anecdotal paintings, reserving his finest satirical comments for the clergy. He regularly exhibited in the Salon, winning medals in 1864, 1867, and 1868, a second class medal in 1878, and an appointment to Chevalier in the Legion of Honor in 1870. Vibert served in the Franco-Prussian War in the artists' battalion with Regnault, Detaille, Clairin, and others. In 1867, he was one of the founders of the watercolor association, Société des aquarellistes français, whose other members included Manet, Doré, Harpignes, Jacque (acc. no. 9), and Detaille. In 1902, he published a two-volume work entitled *La Comédie en peinture* which documented his works and provided explanations for those with ambiguous subjects.
  The Cardinal's Menu depicts a cardinal more concerned with his stomach than with his soul as he engages in a lively discussion with his cook about the intricacies of the day's menu. Between them is a table laden with the makings of a feast with fresh fish and newly-killed fowl. The cabinet in the right background overflows with vegetables and fruit while fresh seafood lies on the tiled floor. The extraordinary clarity of the scene, the sparkling colors Vibert employed, and the reliance on foreground lighting are reminiscent of a theatre set and are a reflection of Vibert's active association with the stage. Vibert's wife was an actress at the Comédie Française and he himself was an accomplished playwright. In 1862, his play *Le Tribune mécanique* opened at the Palais Royale and, in the 1870s, several of his works appeared at the Variétés.

HUGUES MERLE   French, 1822-1881

35 The Lunatic, 1871
Oil on canvas 36½ x 26⅛ inches
Signed LR: Hugues Merle

PROVENANCE: Maynard collection (?); Matthias H. Arnot, 1881; by bequest to the Arnot Art Gallery, 1910.

LITERATURE: *Explication des ouvrages . . . exposés au Palais des Champs-Elysées* (Paris: Imprimerie Nationale, 1873), p. 163, no. 1042 (as "Une Folle"); M. H. Arnot, no. 30 (as "La Folle"); Permanent Collection (1936), no. 35 (as "The Lunatic"); Permanent Collection (1973), p. 120.

  Merle studied under Léon Cogniet at the Ecole des Beaux-Arts. He made his Salon début in 1847 and regularly exhibited his works at the Salons until 1880. He won second class medals in the Salons of 1861 and 1863 and he was made Chevalier of the Legion of Honor in 1866. Merle became quite well-known for his highly-finished, life-size paintings of genre and historical themes. His specialization in sentimental portrayals of women and children led his contemporaries to consider him a rival to W.-A. Bouguereau (see C. H. Stranahan, *A History of French Painting*, NY: Charles Scribner's Sons, 1888, p. 398).
  In the Salon of 1873, Merle exhibited *Une Folle (A Lunatic)*, a blatantly sentimental portrait of a poor woman's pathetic delusion. She sits on the edge of a well, clutching to her chest a log wrapped in a blanket and topped with a baby's bonnet. She looks up and out of the canvas, sympathetically engaging the viewer, whose attention is also drawn to the ominous well hook and rope suspended beside her head. The model's features and grandeur of pose are strongly reminiscent of Merle's similar treatment of the figure in *The Scarlet Letter*, dated 1861 and in the Walters Art Gallery, Baltimore.

JEHAN-GEORGES VIBERT, The Cardinal's Menu; color plate p. 22

HUGUES MERLE, The Lunatic

LUDWIG KNAUS   German, 1829-1910

59 The Child's Funeral, 1856
Oil on canvas 54¼ x 75¾ inches
Signed and dated LR: L. Knaus 1856

PROVENANCE: George I. Seney; Matthias H. Arnot, 1891 (Seney collection sale); by bequest to the Arnot Art Gallery, 1910.

LITERATURE: *Explication des ouvrages... exposés au Palais des Champs-Elysées* (Paris: Charles de Mourgues Freres, 1857), p. 186, no. 1480 (as "Un Convoi funebre"); Seney, pp. 74 and 289, no. 301; "The Seney Sale is Ended," *New York Times*, February 14, 1891; Friedrich von Boetticher, *Malerwerke des 19. Jahrhunderts* (Dresden: 1895), p. 706; Ludwig Pietsch, *Knaus* (Bielefeld and Liepzig: Velhagen and Klasing, 1896), p. 11; M. H. Arnot, no. 68; Permanent Collection (1936), no. 59; Permanent Collection (1973), p. 111, illus. p. 112; *Ludwig Knaus, 1829-1910* (Hanau: Museum Weisbaden and Dr. Hans Peters Verlag, 1979), p. 153, no. 54, illus. p. 152 (as "Funeral Procession in the Woods").

    Ludwig Knaus enjoyed international recognition during his lifetime for his paintings of German peasant genre. Knaus was born in Weisbaden and received his initial art training with O. R. Jacobi, court painter to the Duchy of Nassau. In 1845, he entered the Düsseldorf Academy and studied under Carl Ferdinand Sohn and Wilhelm Schadow. At the Academy Knaus was particularly attracted to the growing trend of naturalism inspired by nineteenth-century Dutch art. In 1848, he joined the *Malkasten*, an "anti-academic" association of landscape and genre painters who were in direct conflict with the Academy's traditional emphasis on historical and religious painting. In a disagreement with Schadow over artistic aims, Knaus left the Academy and set out on his own to study peasant life in Willingshausen, a small village on the Schwalm River to which he returned often in subsequent years and where he established a popular artists' colony. His first large scale genre paintings were favorably received and, his reputation established, he went to Paris in 1853 where his work met with wide acclaim throughout the eight years he remained in France. He regularly won awards at the Salon: a second class in 1853; first class medals in 1855 and 1857; and, in 1859, he was appointed Chevalier of the Legion of Honor. While in Paris, Knaus also made trips to London, Belgium and Italy. He returned to Germany around 1860, settled in Berlin in 1861, moved to Düsseldorf in 1867 and then back to Berlin in 1874 after his appointment as head of the master studio in painting at the Berlin Academy, a post he held for eight years. He spent his later years in Berlin working on private commissions and he frequently traveled to Willingshausen, the Black Forest region, Switzerland, Austria, and to Europe's artistic capitals.
    Knaus' paintings exemplify the art of the Biedermeier period of the 1850s and 1860s. The Biedermeier period was characterized by naturalistic paintings of landscapes and genre scenes which were infused with a sense of nostalgia, gentle humor, and good-natured moralizing. *The Child's Funeral* is an early work painted while Knaus was in Paris and it was exhibited in the Salon of 1857. This large work depicts a funeral procession winding its way through the woods. Led by a young child holding a cross, the convoy is comprised of praying children surrounding their elderly priest, grieving women, and young men as pall bearers. Unlike his colleagues at the Düsseldorf Academy who were known for their brilliant polychromatic canvases, Knaus preferred a warm palette and unified his compostion with a golden tone, occasionally enlivened by contrasting colors of red. The viewer's attention is directed to the foregound figures, all rendered with a fine brush in order to differentiate the children with regard to clothing and hair. The subtle nuances in expressions provide a range in the psychological characterization of the scene: some mourners are too grieved to pray; some are too young to understand; some are distracted or oblivious to the event. The figures in the woods and the background landscape are depicted with a looser brush, providing a less finished yet convincing impression of the outdoor setting.

LUDWIG KNAUS   German, 1829-1910

60 The Old Witch, 1885
Oil on canvas 42 x 29 inches
Signed and dated LR: L Knaus / 1885

PROVENANCE: George I. Seney; Matthias H. Arnot, 1891 (Seney collection sale); by bequest to the Arnot Art Gallery, 1910.

LITERATURE: Seney, pp. 74 and 259, no. 250; "The Seney Sale is Ended," *New York Times*, February 14, 1891; Friedrich von Boetticher, *Malerwerke des 19. Jahrhunderts* (Dresden: 1895), p. 707, no. 48; M. H. Arnot, no. 66; Wilhelm Zils, *Ludwig Knaus* (Munich: 1919), p. 15; Permanent Collection (1936), no. 60; Permanent Collection (1973), p. 112, illus. p. 113; *Ludwig Knaus, 1829-1910* (Hanau: Museum Weisbaden and Dr. Hans Peters Verlag, 1979), p. 172, no. 101 (as "The Village Witch").

    In his later years, Knaus' naturalism was weakened by his reliance upon sentimentality and stagey compositions. *The Old Witch* dates from Knaus' second Berlin period and suffers slightly from the obvious narrative of young boys taunting an old woman, while other children run in terror of the village "witch." The technical brilliance of the work redeems such artistic manipulation. The fluidly-painted landscape of warm browns, greens, and yellows gives the composition a unified richness and illustrates the influence of seventeenth-century Dutch painting on the artist.

LUDWIG KNAUS, The Child's Funeral; color plate p. 25

LUDWIG KNAUS, The Old Witch

FERDINAND THEODOR HILDEBRANDT   German, 1804-1874

57 On the North Sea Coast, n.d.
Oil on canvas 17¹/₈ x 23 inches
Signed LR: F. Hildebrandt

PROVENANCE: Hinman Barrett Hurlbut; Matthias H. Arnot, 1883 (Hurlbut collection sale); by bequest to the Arnot Art Gallery, 1910.

LITERATURE: M. H. Arnot, no. 34; Permanent Collection (1936), no. 57; Permanent Collection (1973), p. 108.

Hildebrandt was born in Stettin and began his art training in 1820 at the Berlin Academy under Wilhelm Schadow. When Schadow left to take charge of the Düsseldorf Academy in 1826, Hildebrandt followed to continue his studies. In 1832, he became a professor at the Düsseldorf Academy and, in time, was named the school's director. Hildebrandt established a reputation as a colorist in his portraits, as well as in his history and genre paintings. He frequently exhibited his works and was elected to memberhip in the Berlin and Vienna academies.

The Düsseldorf Academy dominated German painting in the second quarter of the nineteenth century. Under the direction of Schadow who introduced studies from nature and from live models, Academy-trained artists became popular for their dramatic, vibrantly-colored compositions. After 1840, the reputation of the school rested on its Dutch-influenced genre and still life painting. The increasingly sentimental and folksy bent of the Düsseldorf painters brought domestic fame and international patronage in the 1860s and 1870s. *On the North Sea Coast* illustrates Hildebrandt's affinity for seventeenth-century Dutch painting (compare it, for example, to van de Velde's *A Calm on the Dutch Coast*, acc. no. 50). This modest genre-cum-marine painting presents a view out to sea with ships under sail and one on shore. A family, either newly-arrived or preparing to leave, stands on the shore with baskets and jugs scattered about; other figures are shown working in the masted ship behind them. The low horizon afforded the artist the opportunity to experiment with the delicate hues and muted tones of an overcast sky.

ADOLPHE SCHREYER   German, 1828-1899

65 Mid-day Halt, n.d.
Oil on canvas 17⁷/₈ x 29³/₄ inches
Signed LR: Ad. Schreyer

PROVENANCE: Albert Spencer (?); Matthias H. Arnot, 1879; by bequest to the Arnot Art Gallery, 1910.

LITERATURE: *Catalogue: Loan Exhibition* (Elmira, NY: n.p., 1879), p. 49, no. 102; "The Loan Exhibition," *Elmira Daily Advertiser*, May 31, 1879; M. H. Arnot, no. 4; *St. Louis* (Missouri) *Front Rank*, November 3, 1935; Permanent Collection (1936), no. 65; *Seventh Day Adventists' Youth's Instructor*, October 23, 1956, illus.; Permanent Collection (1973), p. 134.

Schreyer was born in Frankfort, established his reputation in Paris, and enjoyed an international clientele for his Orientalist paintings, landscapes, and military subjects. His initial art training was the genre painter Jacob Becker at Frankfort's Staedel Institute and afterward he studied briefly at the Düsseldorf Academy and traveled to Munich and Stuttgart. In 1849, he moved to Vienna where his acquaintance with the royal family of Thurn und Taxis enabled Schreyer, in the capacity of official artist, to accompany Prince Thurn und Taxis to the Hungarian campaign of 1851 and, in 1855, to the Danube, the eastern part of the Austrian army's field of action in the Crimean War. In 1859 to 1861, Schreyer traveled through North Africa, visiting Egypt, Syria, and Algiers, studying firsthand the language and customs of Bedouin life. He moved to Paris in 1862. Critics favorably compared his paintings to those of Delacroix, Decamps, and Fromentin. Schreyer successfully exhibited his works at the Salons of 1864, 1865 and 1867. At the outbreak of the Franco-Prussian War in 1870, Schreyer returned to Frankfort.

Schreyer's travels in North Africa provided him with a variety of Orientalist subjects that were popular with collectors anxious to purchase scenes of exotic foreign cultures. *Mid-day Halt*, a calm scene of an Arab, his servant, and horses, was atypical for Schreyer who usually depicted Arabs in more aggressive activities, such as riding into battle or preparing for an attack.

FERDINAND THEODOR HILDEBRANDT, On the North Sea Coast

ADOLPHE SCHREYER, Mid-day Halt

FRIEDRICH PETER HIDDEMAN   German, 1829-1892

58 Nobody Was Ever a Master, n.d.
Oil on canvas 26³/₈ x 21⁵/₈ inches
Signed LR: F. Hiddeman

PROVENANCE: Matthias H. Arnot, 1876 (Centennial Exposition purchase); by bequest to the Arnot Art Gallery, 1910.

LITERATURE: *Catalogue: Loan Exhibition* (Elmira, NY: n.p., 1879), p. 49, no. 106; "The Loan Exhibition," *Elmira Daily Advertiser*, May 31, 1879; M. H. Arnot, no. 6; Permanent Collection (1936), no. 58; Permanent Collection (1973), p. 108.

Hiddeman was born in Düsseldorf and studied at the city's Academy under Schadow and Hildebrandt (acc. no. 58). He exhibited his genre paintings internationally and won awards in Vienna in 1873 and at the Centennial Exposition in Philadelphia in 1876.

The Düsseldorf Academy's reputation for a gentle, folksy humor is evident in Hiddeman's *Nobody Was Ever a Master*, depicting an elderly man examining his face for shaving nicks while his young barber looks on. The artist carefully and conscientiously described the colorful details of the setting: the rug-covered floor, the wall cabinet and decorations, the laden tables, and the curtained door. An unidentifiable source from the left lights the two figures, much like a theatrical spotlight, leaving in shadow much of Hiddeman's meticulously-rendered narrative details.

JOHANN GEORG MEYER (MEYER VON BREMEN)   German, 1813-1886

62 The Little Brother Asleep, 1874
Oil on canvas 17¹/₂ x 13⁵/₈ inches
Signed and dated LR: Meyer von Bremen / Berlin 1874

PROVENANCE: Matthias H. Arnot, by 1900; by bequest to the Arnot Art Gallery, 1910.

LITERATURE: *The Masterpieces of German Art*, ed. J. Eugene Reed, A. M., 2 vols. (Philadelphia: Gebbie and Co., [ca. 1884]), 1:28-29; M. H. Arnot, no. 11; Permanent Collection (1936), no. 62; Permanent Collection (1973), p. 120.

Meyer was born in Bremen. In 1833, he traveled to Düsseldorf where he entered the Academy and studied under Carl Ferdinand Sohn. In 1835, he went to the Low Countries on a study trip. After a financially unsuccessful attempt at painting religious subjects, he turned his attention to genre painting, using the seventeenth-century Dutch Masters as an inspiration. In the 1840s, Meyer rapidly established a reputation for himself as the foremost painter of children themes, earning the name "Kindermeyer." In 1852, he moved to Berlin and concentrated solely on small-scale pictures of children, often using his own children as models. Meyer's lyrical scenes of intimate domestic genre were enormously successful, especially with wealthy American collectors.

The Little Brother Asleep, a quiet work celebrating sibling love, was one of Meyer's more popular themes and, beginning in the 1850s, he painted several versions of this particular composition. The influence of the Düsseldorf school is evident in Meyer's foreground stage-like lighting on the figures and crib wrappings and his equally attentive treatment to the still-life details on the cabinet in the background shadows.

FRIEDRICH PETER HIDDEMAN, Nobody Was Ever a Master

JOHANN GEORG MEYER (MEYER VON BREMEN), The Little Brother Asleep

PAUL WEBER   German, 1823-1916

71 Hudson River Landscape, 1854
Oil on canvas 35¹/₁₆ x 49 inches
Signed and dated LR: Paul Weber / Pha. 1854

PROVENANCE: Matthias H. Arnot ; by bequest to the Arnot Art Gallery, 1910.

LITERATURE: Permanent Collection (1936), no. 71; Faison, p. 191, illus.; Permanent Collection (1973), p. 82, illus. p. 84; *Philadelphia: Three Centuries of American Art* (Philadelphia: Philadelphia Museum of Art, 1976), p. 342, no. 295, illus.

Paul Weber was born in Darmstadt, Germany, the son of a court musician. He studied in Frankfort from 1842 to 1844 and in Munich from 1844 to 1848. In 1846 and again in 1847, he toured the Near East in the entourage of Prince Luitpold von Bayern. In 1848, Weber returned to Antwerp to complete his training. Mounting political upheaval in Bavaria and the loss of governmental funding for the arts led Weber to move, in 1849, to the United States. For twelve years, Weber lived in Philadelphia, traveling extensively in the northeast, where he painted a number of scenes in the Catskills and along the Hudson River. He made a brief voyage to Scotland and Germany in 1857. His work was extremely well-received in Philadelphia and he attracted a number of students, including William Stanley Haseltine, William Trost Richards and Edward Moran. In 1861, Weber returned to Darmstadt where he was appointed court painter by Grand Duke of Hesse-Darmstadt. He continued to exhibit his paintings in the United States, London and Germany, winning many awards and honors for his landscapes. Weber died in Munich in 1916.

Hudson River Landscape was painted by Weber while he was living in Philadelphia in 1854, yet this work is a greater reflection of his early art training in Germany rather than of his more recent exposure to the pantheistic philosophy and the highly-focused style of the Hudson River School of painters. Like his American colleagues, Weber was inspired by the landscapes of the northeast. However, he chose not to paint specific, detailed views, preferring instead to approximate a particular site in a formulaic treatment of the landscape. The small town, the island surrounded by the peaceful river, and the mountains hovering protectively in the background were most likely drawn from an actual scene which the artist methodically reorganized to achieve a more pleasing effect. The colors were carefully selected and coordinated for generalized and tonally-unified effects of light and space. Weber's painting suggests a landscape that might just as easily be of the Delaware River or Lackawana country as of the Hudson River valley.

CARL VON MERODE (KARL FREIHERR VON MERODE)   German, 1853-1909

16 The News, n.d.
Oil on panel 8¹/₂ x 6³/₄ inches
Signed LL: C. Merode

PROVENANCE: Wynkoop collection (?); Matthias H. Arnot, by 1900; by bequest to the Arnot Art Gallery, 1910.

LITERATURE: M. H. Arnot, no. 61; Permanent Collection (1936), no. 16; Permanent Collection (1973), p. 140.

Merode was born in Memling, Germany, studied at the Vienna Academy under Fuerbach, and often exhibited in the Berlin Salons. The genre subject of *The News*, two elderly peasant women reading a newspaper while a younger woman looks on, has the folksy appeal that was popular with the bourgeois art-buying public of the late nineteenth century. The colorful embellishments of the scene, the rustic clothing and baskets of produce, distract one's eye from the artist's clumsy handling of anatomy.

PAUL WEBER, Hudson River Landscape

CARL VON MERODE, The News

LUDWIG LOEFFTZ   German, 1845-1910

66 Money Changers, 1884
Oil on canvas 31⁷/₈ x 39¹/₂ inches
Signed and dated LR: L. Loefftz München / 1884

PROVENANCE: Mary Jane Morgan; Marianna Arnot Ogden, 1886 (Morgan collection sale); Matthias H. Arnot, by 1900; by bequest to the Arnot Art Gallery, 1910.

LITERATURE: Morgan, pp. 21 and 48, no. 67; "Buying Fine Paintings," *New York Times*, March 4, 1886; "The Morgan Pictures," *New York Herald*, March 5, 1886; "The Art Sale Finished," *New York Times*, March 6, 1886; M. H. Arnot, no. 45; Permanent Collection (1936), no. 66; Permanent Collection (1973), p. 114.

By the 1860s and 1870s, the Munich school had eclipsed the Düsseldorf Academy in importance and influence. Munich painters featured a heightened sense of naturalism and verisimilitude: their sophisticated Old Master touches and bravura brushwork rapidly gained prominence over the Düsseldorf painters and their old-fashioned folksy realism. In the second half of the century, the Munich school achieved international acclaim for their late Biedermeier style and attracted legions of disciples from all countries to train in their studios.

Loefftz was born in Darmstadt where he was apprenticed at age seventeen to a furniture upholsterer before he decided to pursue art. In 1869, he briefly studied at the Academy in Nuremburg. The following year, he entered the Munich Academy where he studied under the Dutch-influenced genre painter Wilhelm Diez. In 1874, Loefftz was master of his own teaching studio in Munich. Inspired by German and Flemish Old Masters, his meticulous genre paintings attracted many followers and patrons.

Money Changers is typical of Loefftz's highly finished cabinet pictures. An elegantly dressed man in a fur-trimmed coat holds a scale in one hand, tweezers in the other, while another man, most likely a customer, intently watches the balancing act before him. The table where they sit and the wall shelf behind them are strewn with the paraphernalia of the trade: coins, scales, leather sacks, papers and books. Loefftz's virtuoso command of the medium is evident in the life-like recreation of the different textures and finishes in the scene, from the men's haggard faces to the sparkling reflections of the metal surfaces. A curious feature of this painting is the inclusion of another painting depicting St. John the Evangelist and his attribute (the eagle on the wall at the upper right) behind the seated figures. Only a portion of the painting is visible and it is by a decidedly weaker hand, especially when compared to the foreground figures. However, its presence demands consideration. This allusion to the Evangelist suggests the entire genre painting may have a meaning beyond the apparent subject and may imply the theme of Last Judgment and items or souls in the balance. Thus, the entire scene may be interpreted as a variation of a *vanitas* theme, expressing the emptiness of wealth and other worldly possessions.

LUDWIG LOEFFTZ, Money Changers

SIGMUND EGGERT   German, 1839-1896

64 The Village Artist, 1875
Oil on canvas, 30⅛ x 37¾ inches
Signed and dated LR: Eggert Munch 75 (pentimenti)
Signed and dated UR: Sig. Eggert Munch 1875

PROVENANCE: Matthias H. Arnot, 1876 (Centennial Exposition purchase); by bequest to the Arnot Art Gallery, 1910.

LITERATURE: *The Masterpieces of the Centennial International Exhibition*, 3 vols. (Philadelphia: Gebbie and Barrie, 1876-1878; reprint ed., NY: Garland Publishing Co., 1977), vol. 1: Edward Strahan [Earl Shinn], *Fine Arts*, p. 208, illus. p. 153; *Catalogue: Loan Exhibition* (Elmira, NY: n.p., 1879), p. 49, no. 98; "The Loan Exhibition," *Elmira Daily Advertiser*, May 31, 1879; M. H. Arnot, no. 5; Permanent Collection (1936), no. 64; Permanent Collection (1973), p. 104.

Eggert, born in Munich and trained in the city Academy, achieved modest fame for his genre paintings and illustrations. His particular approach, however, had greater affinity with the earlier Biedermier style (Knaus, acc. no. 59) than with the more sophisticated style popular in Munich (Loefftz, acc. no. 66). *The Village Artist* exhibits the good-natured, folksy subject of a provincial artist anxiously showing to the local clerics his finished canvas—probably a religious piece if one is to judge from the works in the background. A young girl, pausing from play, looks at a small portrait of a saint. Like other artists working in the mid-century Beidermeier style (compare, for example, the Düsseldorf artists Hiddeman, acc. no. 58, and Meyer von Bremen, acc. no. 62), the interior setting is presented with a penetrating clarity, with equal attention given to the scene's protagonists as to the incidental details of the setting.
Eggert exhibited this painting at the Centennial Exposition in Philadelphia where it so impressed one reviewer, he selected it as the illustration for "the excellent Munich school, which in a single generation has sprung up into a formidable rival to Paris" (Strahan [Shinn], p. 208).

HEINRICH HIRT   German, active 1870-1890

63 A Story of Olden Time, 1879
Oil on canvas 28⅛ x 21⅜ inches
Signed and dated LL: Heinr. Hirt / Munchen 1879

PROVENANCE: Reid collection (?) ; Matthias H. Arnot, 1882; by bequest to the Arnot Art Gallery, 1910.

LITERATURE: M. H. Arnot, no. 14; *St. Louis* (Missouri) *Front Rank*, November 3, 1935; Permanent Collection (1936), no. 63; *Seventh Day Adventists' Youth's Instructor*, October 23, 1956, illus.; Permanent Collection (1973), p. 109.

Hirt was a minor genre painter active in Munich in the 1870s and 1880s. He exhibited his work in Berlin and Munich.
One of the more popular themes of nineteenth-century German genre painting was domestic tranquility and the strength one derived from one's home. Hirt's painting *A Story of Olden Time* plays on this theme and focuses on the traditions and folk wisdom passed from one generation to another in the depiction of three young girls absorbed in the tales told by an elderly woman. The rosary the old woman clutches on her lap, the well-scrubbed girls, and the sleeping cat on the threshold of the door are evidence that these humble folk are healthy, safe, and contented.

SIGMUND EGGERT, The Village Artist

HEINRICH HIRT, A Story of Olden Time

LUIGI ZUCCOLI   Italian, 1815-1876

56 The Betrothal, ca. 1876
Oil on canvas 15⅝ x 18¾ inches
Signed LR: Luigi Zuccoli / Roma

PROVENANCE: Matthias H. Arnot, 1876; by bequest to the Arnot Art Gallery, 1910.

LITERATURE: *Catalogue: Loan Exhibition* (Elmira, NY: n.p., 1879), p. 40, no. 105; "The Loan Exhibition," *Elmira Daily Advertiser*, May 31, 1879; M. H. Arnot, no. 1; Permanent Collection (1936), no. 56; Permanent Collection (1973), p. 140; *Italian Paintings: 1850-1910* (Williamstown, MA: Clark Art Institute, 1982), p. 80.

Zuccoli was born in Milan where his genre paintings of Italian peasant life earned him election to the Brera Academy in his native city. He lived in England from 1860 to 1865 and his works were exhibited at the Royal Academy in London from 1864 to 1871.

The tradition of genre painting in Milan was established in the polished, sentimental peasant subjects of the Induno brothers. *The Betrothal* illustrates Zuccoli's connection to this tradition in the highly finished treatment of a peasant family basking in the glow of a marital engagement. A young man stands at the left holding a ring and looking at his intended, who holds a red-beaded necklace in her hand. An elderly man, his wife, and other daughter witness the exchange, the old man raising his glass in a silent toast. Zuccoli renders this interaction with a superficial sentimental gloss, his emphasis instead is on presenting the material details of the clean, but untidy world of peasant life. The rough-textured fabrics, brick floor and white-washed walls, and bits of crockery are painted with an almost photographic precision.

ROBERTO RASINELLI   Italian, active 1873-1877

24 The Love Letter, 1873
Oil on canvas 12⅞ x 6¾ inches
Signed and dated LC: Rasinelli / Roma 73

PROVENANCE: Matthias H. Arnot, 1873; by bequest to the Arnot Art Gallery, 1910.

LITERATURE: M. H. Arnot, no. 26; Permanent Collection (1936), no. 24; Permanent Collection (1973), p. 126; *Italian Paintings, 1850-1910* (Williamstown, MA: Clark Art Institute, 1982), p. 80.

Born in Rome, Rasinelli received his training in art at the Academy of St. Luke and frequently exhibited his works in Naples, Rome, Florence, and Bologna. In style, Rasinelli's work has much in common with the Neapolitan movement called the School of Resina, active in the mid-1860s. More of an association of artists than a distinct school, the anti-academic movement was founded by Marco De Gregorio whose preference for realism and *plein air* painting influenced the following generation of painters.

Rasinelli combined his academic training with the more progressive ideas of the School of Resina in his genre paintings. *The Love Letter* depicts a woman leaning out her window and dangling a red ribbon, perhaps taken from her paramour's recent letter. The ambiguous subject is enlivened by the artist's concern for naturalism and his observation of light and shadow. The strong mid-day sun broadly defines the flat planes of the buildings while the overhanging shade filters and diffuses the light to illuminate the woman.

LUIGI ZUCCOLI, The Betrothal

ROBERTO RASINELLI, The Love Letter

EMILIO SANCHEZ-PERRIER   Spanish, 1855-1907

36 By the River (Alcala), n.d.
Oil on panel 17½ x 24 inches
Signed LR: E. Sanchez-Perrier / Alcala
Inscribed verso UR: El Zacatin / (Alcala)

PROVENANCE: Samuel Putnam Avery, Jr.; Matthias H. Arnot, by 1900; by bequest to the Arnot Art Gallery, 1910.

LITERATURE: M. H. Arnot, no. 62; Permanent Collection (1936), no. 36; Permanent Collection (1973), p. 132, illus. p. 133; Christopher Kuhl, "The Spanish Influence: A Visual Legacy," *Horizon* (December 1987):17-52, illus. p. 22.

    The landscapist Sanchez-Perrier was born in Seville and is known for his paintings of his home city and native country. Like many Spanish artists of his generation, he regularly worked and exhibited in France where he achieved modest success, including an honorable mention in the Salon of 1886 and a silver medal in 1889.
    By the River was painted at Alcala, a small city approximately twenty miles east of Madrid and on the river Henares. The artist has selectively edited the scene to obtain compositional balance, cutting the boat on the left, the top portion of the trees, and their reflection on the water below. Such croppings of scenery is characteristic of Sanchez-Perrier's landscapes and his combination of hard and soft focus of details gives his works an extraordinary, almost unsettling sense of realism. Note, for example, the crisp lines of the tree limbs as contrasted to the blurred appearance of the surrounding bushes, an effect reminiscent of long-exposure photographs which combine a high resolution for static objects with less focused areas of moving objects. Some scholars have commented on this "photographic" quality in his landscapes and suggest the artist may have employed calotypes or some other nineteenth-century photographic technique as a model (see Marcus B. Burke, *A Selection of Masterworks from the Meadows Museum*, Dallas: Southern Methodist University, 1986, p. 13).

LUIS RICCARDO FALERO   Spanish, 1851-1896

69 The Syrian Music Girl, 1878
Oil on canvas 16¼ x 9½ inches
Signed and dated LR: FALERO / 1878

PROVENANCE: Hinman Barrett Hurlbut; Matthias H. Arnot, 1883 (Hurlbut collection sale); by bequest to the Arnot Art Gallery, 1910.

LITERATURE: M. H. Arnot, no. 46; Permanent Collection (1936), no. 69; Permanent Collection (1973), p. 105.

    Falero was born in Granada, traveled to Paris to study art, and later settled in London. He enjoyed modest success for his facility in a range of subjects: marine landscapes of his native Spain, literary paintings, and Orientalist subjects, many of which featured nude or partially nude women.
    The Syrian Music Girl is the most explicitly sexual painting Matthias Arnot owned. Under the thinly-veiled pretense of Orientalist exotica, Falero presents a partially-robed girl languidly playing a stringed instrument while coyly gazing at her audience.

A. E. FABRI   Italian (?), active 1872-1903

23 The Mirror, 1872
Oil on panel 10⅛ x 6⅞ inches
Signed and dated LL: A. E. FABRI / Roma 1872

PROVENANCE: Matthias H. Arnot, ca. 1872-1873; by bequest to the Arnot Art Gallery, 1910.

LITERATURE: M. H. Arnot, no. 8; Permanent Collection (1936), no. 23; Permanent Collection (1973), p. 104.

    The late nineteenth-century public was intrigued by the exotic Near East and its decadent lifestyle. Painters such as Gérôme (acc. nos. 12 and 13) found success with meticulously detailed scenes based on their travels which informed the public on the dress, setting, and customs of foreign peoples. Lesser artists also found an audience for their paintings which assumed an Orientalist style without the substance. Fabri's Arab maiden, dressed in thin, multi-colored scarves and looking admiringly at herself in a mirror is one such work geared more for titillation than education. Though the provocative pose and exotic trappings may have piqued the buyer's interest, it does not hide the artist's less than confident handling of anatomy and composition.

EMILIO SANCHEZ-PERRIER, By the River (Alcala); color plate p. 4

LUIS RICCARDO FALERO, The Syrian Music Girl

A.E. FABRI, The Mirror

MARTIN RICO Y ORTEGA   Spanish, 1833-1908

22 Santa Euphemia on the Lagoon, Venice, n.d.
Oil on canvas 20⅞ x 30 inches
Signed CR: Rico

PROVENANCE: Wynkoop collection (?) ; Matthias H. Arnot, by 1900; by bequest to the Arnot Art Gallery, 1910.

LITERATURE: M. H. Arnot, no. 56; Permanent Collection (1936), no. 22; Permanent Collection (1973), p. 128, illus.

    Rico's small luminous landscapes of French, Spanish, and Italian views won him the appointment to Chevalier of the Legion of Honor in 1878. In his home city of Madrid, Rico received training from the classicist Vicente Camaron y Melia before enrolling in the Royal Academy at San Fernando under the landscape painter Genaro Pérez Villaamils. Cautioned against working directly from nature, Rico copied the landscape prints of Alexandre Calame and Hubert Robert. Around 1859, he received a scholarship to study in France. Though Daubigny (acc. no. 2) rejected him as a student, Rico stayed in France and began painting in oils and watercolors out of doors. In 1860, he traveled to Switzerland to work with Calame who further encouraged him to paint *en plein air*. He also traveled to England in 1862 to study Turner's work. Rico stayed in Paris after his scholarship expired in the mid-1860s, supporting himself with wood engravings and small paintings of historical genre subjects in the manner of Meissonier (acc. nos. 14 and 15). He soon befriended the fellow Spaniard and genre painter Mariano Fortuny, who had arrived in Paris in 1866, and the two often painted together and traveled to Rome in 1872. Between 1874 and 1878, Rico traveled through France, Italy, and Spain. The sixteen landscapes he produced were exhibited to much acclaim and awarded a third class medal at the Exposition Universelle in 1878. He won a silver medal in the Exposition Universelle in 1889.

    For the last two decades of his life, Rico spent increasing amounts of time in Venice and became known for his paintings of the city produced from a gondola on the canal. *Santa Euphemia on the Lagoon, Venice* was painted on the water. The square tower of Santa Euphemia is visible behind the retaining wall and trees to the left of center. The shimmering water and the almost eerie clarity of the brilliant colors reveals Rico's sensitivity to the unique atmosphere and light of his adopted city.

MARTIN RICO Y ORTEGA, Santa Euphemia on the Lagoon, Venice

JOHN GLOVER   English, 1767-1849

26 Borrowdale, Cumberland, 1827
Watercolor on paper 8½ x 11¹/₁₆ inches
Signed and dated on mount LR: J. Glover 1827
Inscribed on mount LL: Borrowdale Cumberland

PROVENANCE: Alexander, tenth Duke of Hamilton, by 1852; by descent to William, twelfth Duke of Hamilton, 1863; Matthias H. Arnot, 1882 (Hamilton Palace collection sale); by bequest to the Arnot Art Gallery, 1910.

LITERATURE: Hamilton 1, p. 143, no. 1105; "The Hamilton Palace Sale," *London Times*, July 10, 1882; Hamilton 2, p. 145, and no. 1105; M. H. Arnot, no. 37; Permanent Collection (1936), no. 26; Permanent Collection (1973), p. 107, illus.

During his lifetime, Glover was an highly successful landscape painter and, of his generation, he was considered to be the main rival to Turner. Glover was born to a poor farming family in Houghton-on-the-Hill, Leicestershire. He had little formal training, studying briefly with John "Warwick" Smith and later with William Payne of Plymouth. By 1786, he was employed as a writing teacher at a school in Appleby and, during his eight year tenure, he completed several commissions for topographical studies of local interest. In 1794, he moved to Lichfield to teach drawing and submitted three landscape views to the Royal Academy the following year. Glover moved to London in 1804 or 1805, though he continued his popular teaching practice in the Midlands. He was one of the original members of the Old Water-Color Society, founded in 1804, and he served as its president in 1813. He was a regular contributor to the Society's exhibitions, selling most of the works he submitted, and he continued to exhibit his oils at the Royal Academy exhibitions. Glover's influence and his enthusiasm for oil painting led to changes at the Society and, after 1812, it was renamed the Society of Painters in Oil and Watercolors. Glover exhibited one of his landscapes at the Salon of 1814 in Paris, winning an award, and over the next two years he traveled the continent making landscape sketches. After attempting unsuccessfully to gain election to the Royal Academy, Glover opened his own gallery in 1820. He displayed his pictures alongside works by Claude (acc. no. 32), confidant that his works would not suffer through the comparison. This led to Constable's sarcastic dismissal of Glover as "our English Claude" (see *Magazine of the Fine Arts*, 1821, pp. 126-128). In 1824, Glover was a founding member of the Society of British Artists. In 1831, Glover and his family emigrated to Tasmania where he remained until his death.

Glover's landscapes are closer to the concepts of ideal landscape painting in the tradition of Claude than they are to naturalistic landscapes. Glover combines carefully arranged compositions, the preferance for a limited palette, and the technique of using underlying tints rather than painting directly in local color. He became well known for his idiosyncratic mannerism of rendering foliage with a 'split brush': he twisted the hairs of his brush into two or more points, resulting in little parallel strokes which suggest sun-dappled and gently moving masses of leaves. The Lake District was a favorite region for sketching and Cumberland, in particular, was a recurring subject in Glover's landscapes. *Borrowdale, Cumberland* is a typical illustration of his approach to landscape sketches. Completing the sky first, Glover painted the background in cool washes of blue and grey tints made of indigo ink, reserving the warmer tones for the foreground. Local colors, orange and green for the landscape and blue for the meandering river in this particular work, were added after the scene was fully sketched.

JOHN GLOVER, Borrowdale, Cumberland

GEORGE HENRY BOUGHTON   English, 1833-1905

27 Winter Landscape, ca. 1855 (?)
Oil on board 13⁷/₈ x 18³/₁₆ inches
n.s.

PROVENANCE: Matthias H. Arnot, by 1900; by bequest to the Arnot Art Gallery, 1910.

LITERATURE: M. H. Arnot, no. 28; Permanent Collection (1936), no. 27; Permanent Collection (1973), p. 92.

Boughton was the son of a farmer from Norwich, England, who moved his family to America in 1834 and settled in the area of Albany, New York. Self-taught by copying engravings, Boughton opened a studio in Albany in 1852, advertising himself as a landscape painter, and he also began to exhibit his works at the American Art Union and the National Academy. In 1856, he briefly visited Great Britain, touring the Lake District, Ireland, and Scotland. In 1860, he traveled to Paris where he studied informally with Edouard May and Edouard Frere. He moved to London in 1862 and his submissions to the exhibitions at the British Institution and the Royal Academy drew considerable attention. Like Whistler, he considered himself more English than American. Though he was elected to the National Academy in New York in 1871, Boughton preferred to exhibit his work in the English section of Memorial Hall at the Centennial Exposition in Philadelphia in 1876. Ironically, much of Boughton's subject matter were anecdotal scenes drawn from American literature and history, especially the Puritan and Knickerbocker periods. In the early 1880s, a trip to the Netherlands signaled a change in Boughton's work and he painted scenes based on his travels which he published in 1885 as *Sketching Rambles in Holland*. Boughton continued to receive due recognition for his sentimental scenes and, in 1879, he was elected Associate in the Royal Academy, gaining full membership in 1896.

Typical of Boughton's work are paintings of modest format with small figures placed against the background landscape. Usually there is a pretty woman or quaint bit of architecture. In *Winter Landscape*, a woman and a young boy are seen walking in a snow-covered landscape in front of a small church. This picturesque scene is conscientiously organized with the foreground trees leading the viewer to the figures and the church in the middleground left and then off to the distant horizon at the right. The painting appears to date from the early part of Boughton's career, perhaps even prior to his first trip to Britain, as it relies more on conventional landscape traditions and less on the charming sentimental narratives that characterize his later productions.

GEORGE HENRY BOUGHTON   English, 1833-1905

28 Morning, n.d.
Oil on canvas 28¹/₂ x 15¹/₂ inches
Initialed LL: G.H.B.

PROVENANCE: Albert Spencer (?); Matthias H. Arnot, 1879; by bequest to the Arnot Art Gallery, 1910.

LITERATURE: *Catalogue: Loan Collection* (Elmira, NY: n.p., 1879), p. 49, no. 113; "The Loan Exhibition," *Elmira Daily Advertiser*, May 31, 1879; M. H. Arnot, no. 9; Permanent Collection (1936), no. 28; Permanent Collection (1973), p. 92.

Morning signals a distinct change in approach by the self-taught landscape artist from Albany and most likely dates from Boughton's English years. The pink gowned figure gazing abstractly at the ground in front of her appears to be Boughton's highly abbreviated version of Aurora, the goddess of the Dawn, often called "rosy-fingered" by Homer. In Boughton's painting, she stands nonchalantly beside a pool of water leaning on a deep rose-colored wrap draped on a boulder. The flowing pink gown reveals the body underneath and suggests the artist had recently had the opportunity to study Greek sculpture, particularly the Elgin Marbles, the pediment sculptures from the Parthenon on view at the British Museum.

GEORGE HENRY BOUGHTON, Winter Landscape

GEORGE HENRY BOUGHTON, Morning

ERSKINE NICOL   Scottish, 1825-1904

29 Under a Cloud, 1876
Oil on canvas 30³/₄ x 39³/₄ inches
Signed and dated LR: Nicol 1876

PROVENANCE: Matthias H. Arnot, by 1900; by bequest to the Arnot Art Gallery, 1910.

LITERATURE: M. H. Arnot, no. 48; Permanent Collection (1936), no. 29; Permanent Collection (1973), p. 124.

    Nicol was born in Leith outside Edinburgh. In his youth, he worked as a house painter and later decided to apply himself to serious painting by enrolling in the Trustee Academy at Edinburgh. He traveled to Ireland, teaching drawing and painting portraits in Dublin and where, as Clarence Cook noted, he gathered material for "those studies of Irish character that have made his name so well known to lovers of humor on both sides of the Atlantic" (Clarence Cook, *Art and Artists of Our Time*, 3 vols., NY: Selmar Hess, 1888, 3:117). He returned to Edinburgh where his paintings earned him election to the Royal Scottish Academy in 1859. Nicol moved to London in 1863 where he was elected Associate Member of the Royal Academy in 1867 and later full Academician.
    Nicol's genre subjects of contemporary life are devoted to his humorous observations of Scottish and Irish characters. His paintings were known by a wide audience as his works were frequently engraved and widely exhibited in Britain and America. Among them are several works from a private collection which were loaned to the National Academy exhibitions, as well as Nicol's own submissions to the Centennial Exposition in Philadelphia in 1876. *Under a Cloud* is one of Nicol's Irish genre subjects. As noted by the artist:

> *My picture represents Paddy under a cloud, as he has been, more or less, especially more, ever since I knew him. He is represented "after" relating the old, old story of bad crops, short rents, if any, with all the other ills that Irish peasant flesh is heir to, to his landlord, who has borne with him till his patience is thread bare. It does not follow however that the cloud is either so dense as it seems, or is represented, either by Paddy or me, but it is often suitable, frequently serviceable and always available, it is meant to be a simple story of very every day Irish life.* (Excerpt from a now unlocated letter from the artist to Matthias Arnot reproduced in Arnot's collection catalogue.)

PIERRE HENRI THEODORE TETAR VAN ELVEN   Dutch, 1831-1908

44 Street Scene in a Flemish Town, n.d.
Oil on canvas 15⁷/₈ x 12¹³/₁₆ inches
Signed LR: T. van Elven / [illeg.]
Inscribed LL: [illeg.]

PROVENANCE: Hinman Barrett Hurlbut ; Matthias H. Arnot, 1883 (Hurlbut collection sale); by bequest to the Arnot Art Gallery, 1910.

LITERATURE: M. H. Arnot, no. 32; Permanent Collection (1936), no. 44; Permanent Collection (1973), p. 137.

    Tetar van Elven was born in Amsterdam where he later received art training from Jan-Baptiste Tetar van Elven. He specialized in street views or cityscapes based on his travels around the continent and he exhibited his works in the Paris Salons of 1861 and 1865.
    Street Scene in a Flemish Town, to use Matthias Arnot's title, is characteristic of his work. It is a modest genre piece of a northern European street scene with steeply roofed masonry buildings, a church on the left, residential houses on the right, and a few incidental figures walking about.

ERSKINE NICOL, Under a Cloud

PIERRE HENRI THEODORE TETAR VAN ELVEN, Street Scene in a Flemish Town

EUGENE JOSEPH VERBOECKHOVEN   Flemish, 1799-1881

45 Interior of a Barn with Sheep, 1873
Oil on panel 11³/₄ x 9¹⁵/₁₆ inches
Signed LR: Eugene Verboeckhoven / [illeg.] 1873
Inscribed verso LC: Je soussigné Dicter que / le tableau à contra est / original. / Eugène Verboeckhoven / Schaubilds bz Bruxelles / 1873

PROVENANCE: Matthias H. Arnot, by 1879 from the artist; by bequest to the Arnot Art Gallery, 1910.

LITERATURE: *Catalogue: Loan Exhibition* (Elmira, NY: n.p., 1879), p. 49, no. 100; "The Loan Exhibition," *Elmira Daily Advertiser*, May 31, 1879; M. H. Arnot, no. 2; Permanent Collection (1936), no. 45; Permanent Collection (1973), p. 139.

EUGENE JOSEPH VERBOECKHOVEN   Flemish, 1799-1881

46 Watching the Flock, 1861
Oil on canvas 29 x 24¹/₄ inches
Signed and dated LL: Eugene Verboeckhoven / 1861

PROVENANCE: Samuel Putnam Avery, Jr.; Matthias H. Arnot, by 1900; by bequest to the Arnot Art Gallery, 1910.

LITERATURE: M. H. Arnot, no. 58; Permanent Collection (1936), no. 46; Permanent Collection (1973), p. 139.

    Verboeckhoven's talents as a sculptor, printmaker and painter of portraits, landscapes, and animal scenes were encouraged at an early age by his father Barthélemy Verboeckhoven (1754-1840), a sculptor who also taught Eugène's brother Louis (1802-1889), and who later made a name for himself as a marine painter. Eugène's skill in sculpture endowed his paintings with the appearance of physical presence and solidity of form. His sympathetic portrayals of animals earned him many patrons in England and America, especially after his trip to London where he was permitted to study in the royal menagerie. He exhibited widely, including London, Brussels and St. Petersburg, his reputation attracting a large number of students and followers to his Brussels studio. At the Paris Salons, he won a second class medal in 1824, first class in 1841, and third class in 1855. By the end of his life, he had accumulated several international honors: France's Cross of the Legion of Honor; and appointment to the Order of Leopold of Belgium; and the Iron Cross of Germany.
    Verboeckhoven excelled in painting sheep and most of his works incorporate one or more of the animals in composed pastoral landscapes rendered in clear, fresh colors. *Interior of a Barn with Sheep* and *Watching the Flock* are characteristic of his loving depiction of the forms and textures of animals and his empathetic rendering of their "emotions." For example, in *Watching the Flock*, note the attentive, paternalistic gaze of the dog looking down upon his charges and the protective bearing of the reclining sheep over her two lambs.

EUGENE JOSEPH VERBOECKHOVEN, Interior of a Barn with Sheep

EUGENE JOSEPH VERBOECKHOVEN, Watching the Flock

ROBERT STREET   American, 1796-1865

72 Zachary Taylor, 1850
Oil on canvas 30 x 25¼ inches
Signed and dated CR: Robt. Street / 1850

PROVENANCE: Matthias H. Arnot, by 1879; by bequest to the Arnot Art Gallery, 1910.

LITERATURE: *Catalogue: Loan Exhibition* (Elmira, NY: n.p., 1879), p. 49, no. 99; "The Loan Exhibition," *Elmira Daily Advertiser*, May 31, 1879; Permanent Collection (1936), no. 72; Permanent Collection (1973), p. 70.

       Street was born in Germantown, Pennsylvania, and spent most of his career in the Philadelphia area where he established his reputation and supported himself as a portrait painter. He exhibited his works at the Pennsylvania Academy of Fine Arts between 1815 and 1817 and, in 1824, he had an exhibition in Washington, D.C. of his portrait commissions of prominent men. In 1840, he held an exhibition of over two hundred of his historical paintings, landscapes, and portraits at the Artists' Fund Hall in Philadelphia.
       It is unlikely Matthias Arnot personally acquired this painting for his collection. He was only seventeen years old when this painting was created and, more significantly, works by American artists are rare in his collection. Boughton (acc. nos. 27 and 28) was an American expatriate who achieved fame and success in Europe, while Ives (acc. no. 307) and Mozier (acc. no. 308) were sculptors living in Italy whose works Arnot acquired early in his collecting career and before he gave the collection a specific focus. This Street painting is more likely to have been commissioned or purchased by his father or another family member, hung in the Arnot home, remaining there after Matthias Arnot assumed title to the property.

GUISEPPE MAZZOLINI   Italian, 19th century

70 Madonna and Child with St. Ann
Oil on canvas 39 x 29¾ inches
n.s.
Inscribed verso UC: M.R.S. Palmer / New York (inscribed tag)
Inscribed verso CC: Guiseppe Mazzolini diptuse / Roma 186 (preprinted tag)

PROVENANCE: Richard Suydham Palmer, ca. 1870; Matthias H. Arnot; by bequest to the Arnot Art Gallery, 1910.

LITERATURE: Permanent Collection (1936), no. 70; Permanent Collection (1973), p. 118.

       Mazzolini was an artist working in Rome in the last part of the nineteenth century who painted, usually on commission, uninspired copies or pastiches of works by Italian or Flemish masters.
       Richard Suydham Palmer was the husband of Matthias Arnot's younger sister, Fanny. He may have accompanied Arnot on his first trip to Rome in 1869-1870 where he might have commissioned this work, or he may have asked Arnot to purchase a work for him. The subject certainly had special significance to the Palmers: in the two years prior to the Rome journey, Fanny Arnot Palmer had given birth to two sons.

O.T. CYPHAS (?)   Russian (?), 19th century

68 The Chimney Sweep, n.d.
Oil on canvas 25 x 19⅝ inches
Signed LL: [illeg.]

PROVENANCE: Matthias H. Arnot, 1876 (Centennial Exposition purchase); by bequest to the Arnot Art Gallery, 1910.

LITERATURE: *Catalogue: Loan Exhibition* (Elmira, NY: n.p., 1879), p. 49, no. 112 (as by "Gypad"); M. H. Arnot, no. 22; Permanent Collection (1936), no. 68; Permanent Collection (1973), no. 99.

ROBERT STREET, Zachary Taylor

GUISEPPE MAZZOLINI, Madonna and Child with St. Ann

O.T. CYPHAS, The Chimney Sweep

ANTOINE LOUIS BARYE   French, 1796-1875

319 Stag, n.d.
Bronze 19¼ x 20½ x 9¾ inches
Inscribed on base, top right: susse fecies-editeurs [illeg.] / BARYE

PROVENANCE: Matthias H. Arnot, by 1879; by bequest to the Arnot Art Gallery, 1910.

LITERATURE: *Catalogue: Loan Exhibition* (Elmira, NY: n.p., 1879), p. 43, no. 1782; Permanent Collection (1973), p. 156.

Barye was the pre-eminent *animalier* of the nineteenth century and his works in bronze and watercolor received much official recognition as well as popular support throughout his life. Born to a goldsmith in Lyons, Barye was exposed to his father's craft at an early age, and by the time he was thirteen, he apprenticed to a metal engraver of military equipment in the Fourier foundry. Barye also worked in the shop of Guillaume Biennais, goldsmith to Napoleon and the French crown, and made iron dies for metal stamping. He was drafted into the military in 1812 and, after his service, his interests were increasingly drawn to the fine arts of painting and sculpture. In 1816, he studied briefly with the neo-classical sculptor F.J. Bosio and then with the Romantic painter Baron Gros. From 1818 to 1823, he was a student at the Ecole des Beaux-Arts, which afforded him the opportunity to study works from antiquity, the Renaissance, the Baroque, and the more recent neo-classical period. From 1823 to 1831, Barye worked for the goldsmith Fauconnier and studied the animals in the menagerie of the Jardin des Plantes, the specimens and skeltons in the Musée d'Anatomie Comparée, and observed dissections of animals. His notorious entry to the Salon of 1831, *Tiger Devouring a Gavial of the Ganges*, won him a second class medal and established his reputation as a mature and daring sculptor. Subsequently, Barye received official endorsement and commissions from the Orléanist government, including the purchase of his monumental work *Lion Crushing Serpent* from the Salon of 1833, which was cast in bronze by the crown and placed in the garden of the Tuileries palace. In 1848, he was made director of plaster casting in the Louvre and curator of the gallery of plaster casts. In 1854, he was appointed master of zoological drawing in the Musée d'Histoire Naturelle of Paris where, in 1863, Rodin studied under him. He was appointed Chevalier of the Legion of Honor in 1833, received the Cross of the Legion of Honor in 1855, and was named to the Institut de France in 1868.

Early on, Barye recognized the growing patronage of the general public and he began creating small bronzes suitable for the newly rich bourgeoisie. In 1839, he began a workshop to make and market his works and, in 1840, he formed a partnership with Emile Martin to support the artist's various foundries, salesrooms, and ateliers. Barye's company went bankrupt in 1846, but his success is evident in the proliferation of his work, though at the price of uneven craftsmanship. After his death, the Barbedienne foundry purchased 125 models at the artist's estate sale and produced casts of Barye's work well into the twentieth century. Other foundries produced unauthorized editions of variable quality.

Barye was renowned for his dramatic representations of animals, in particular, the feline predator with its prey. His sense of realism combined his scientific understanding of animal anatomy with his flair for capturing the energy and tension of a dramatic instant, sacrificing neither the design nor the rhythm of the work. The elegant bronze sculpture in the Arnot collection is a twelve-point stag poised with his leg raised and head arched back and looking to the left. The curve of the animal's antlers, repeated in the more angular lines of the legs, define the work as a system of lines and curves moving through three-dimensional space.

ANTOINE LOUIS BARYE, Stag

GUILLAUME DENIERE   French, active 1814-1860

301 **William Tell**, n.d.
Bronze 24½ x 9½ x 8½ inches
Inscribed on base, top front: Deniere
PROVENANCE: Matthias H. Arnot; by bequest to the Arnot Art Gallery, 1910.
LITERATURE: Permanent Collection (1973), p. 157.

Little is known about Denière although he was active in the Salons between 1814-1860. This work depicts William Tell, the legendary archer, wearing a suit of armor with a quiver of arrows slung on his hip. He is attempting to string his bow and the rope wrapped around his hand originally extended to the base, traveled under his foot, and hooked to the end of the bow. A bronze piece based upon a single literary figure, such as Denière's *William Tell*, was well suited to the medium of sculpture; complex narrative themes involving many figures and events were more successfully handled in the flexible medium of painting.

ANONYMOUS   French, 19th century

300 **Venus de Milo**
Bronze 39½ x 12½ x 12 inches
Inscribed on base, top left: Fic Sauvage Reduction / Paris
PROVENANCE: Matthias H. Arnot, by 1879; by bequest to the Arnot Art Gallery, 1910.
LITERATURE: *Catalogue: Loan Exhibition* (Elmira, NY: n.p., 1879), p. 44, no. 1822; "The Loan Exhibition," *Elmira Daily Advertiser*, May 30, 1879; Permanent Collection (1973), p. 156.

Reductions and bronze copies of famous sculptures were popular parlor decorations in Victorian American homes, advertising the owner's cultured taste and aesthetic refinement. Such *objets d'art* were readily available: many department stores, such as John Wanamakers in Philadelphia, often featured reproductions of art, as well as original works, in their home furnishings department (see Remy G. Saisselin, *The Bourgeois and the Bibelot*, New Brunswick: Rutgers University Press, 1984, pp. 32-50). It would not be surprising to learn that Matthias Arnot acquired his bronze reproduction of the Venus de Milo from such a source, perhaps even from Wanamakers while he was in Philadelphia to view the Centennial Exposition.

GUILLAUME DENIERE, William Tell

ANONYMOUS, Venus de Milo

CHAUNCEY BRADLEY IVES   American, 1810-1894

307 John Arnot, Sr., 1870
Marble 26½ x 22½ x 13¼ inches
Inscribed and dated on back, left: C. B. IVES / FECIT / ROMAE 1870

PROVENANCE: Matthias H. Arnot, 1870; by bequest to the Arnot Art Gallery, 1910.
LITERATURE: Permanent Collection (1973), p. 149.

In the nineteenth century, America's lack of history, as well as its lack of cultural and artistic heritage, forced many of the young nation's artists to travel to Europe for training and inspiration. These European apprenticeships had several advantages: proximity to the art treasures of Europe and the opportunity for American artists to judge their work in relation to the standards set by Europe's art academies. In addition, European study increased the chance to obtain patronage from affluent American tourists who were more supportive of native artists abroad (after the artists had been properly inculated in European culture) than at home. Colonies of American artists could be found all over the continent: Paris, Düsseldorf, Munich, and especially Rome and Florence. Sculptors were particularly attracted to Italy for its sculptural tradition, as well as for technical necessities, such as the availability of materials and skilled stone cutters.

Chauncey Bradley Ives was born in Hamden, Connecticut. After an apprenticeship in woodcarving, he decided to become a sculptor rather than a craftsman, studying first with Hezekiah Augur and producing portrait busts. In 1841, he took his early works to Boston where they were exhibited at the Atheneum to favorable review. He opened a studio in New York City and produced a number of portraits. Ill health prompted him to seek a warmer and, perhaps, more stimulating climate so he sailed to Italy, arriving in Florence in 1844. Initially, portrait commissions were sparse, thereby enabling Ives to study Florence's treasures and which inspired him to attempt more idealized works based on literary subjects. In 1851, he moved to Rome where the naturalism of his early works gave way to an increased neo-classicism under the influence of Roman art. Ives' idealized figures, such as *Pandora*, *Rebecca at the Well*, and *Undine*, were enormously popular with American public and the artist produced replicas to satisfy collectors' demands. His reputation increased his portraiture commissions, especially from wealthy tourists abroad who visited his studio and Ives' blend of naturalism and neo-classicism only added to his popularity. As Wayne Craven noted:

> . . . Ives managed to avoid a dry literalism, and somehow smoothed off much of the coarseness of the American physiognomy; he ignored the unessential details and emphasized his patrons' handsomer features, which of course pleased them immensely. (Wayne Craven, *Sculpture in America*, NY: Thomas Y. Crowell, 1968, p. 287.)

Except for occasional trips back to America to exhibit and sell his works and to obtain commissions, Ives remained in Rome until his death in 1894.

Like other wealthy tourists, when Matthias Arnot was in Italy in 1869-1870, he visited the studios of America's prominent sculptors to observe their latest artistic efforts. By 1870, Ives was already quite successful and well-known for his ideal figural subjects and his portrait commissions. Arnot probably needed no other recommendation and commissioned Ives to do a portrait bust of his father. John Arnot, Sr., the ambitious, self-made millionaire from New England, is depicted in a Roman toga. The face is of an aging man with fleshy skin and furrowed brow, but with no loss of command, judging from the focused gaze of the eyes and the firmly set mouth.

JOSEPH MOZIER   American, 1812-1870

308 The Wept of Wish-ton-Wish, 1869
Marble 51½ x 21½ x 17 inches
Inscribed and dated on base, right: J. MOZIER. Sc. / ROME 1869
Inscribed on base, front: THE WEPT OF WISH-TON-WISH

PROVENANCE: Matthias H. Arnot, 1869-1870; by bequest to the Arnot Art Gallery, 1910.
LITERATURE: William H. Gerdts, "Marble and Nudity," *Art in America* 59 (May-June, 1971), p. 62, illus. p. 61; Permanent Collection (1973), p. 151.

Mozier was born in Burlington, Vermont. He was already a successful New York merchant when his desire to be a sculptor led him to sail to Europe in 1845. He opened a studio in Rome where he worked until his death in 1870. Mozier built a reputation for his ideal figures drawn from literary sources and, like Ives (acc. no. 307), reproduced the more successful ones, such as *The Wept of Wish-ton-Wish*, in smaller replicas to satisfy public demand. *The Wept of Wish-ton-Wish* depicts the Indian heroine of the James Fenimore Cooper novel of the same title, first published in 1829. The story focuses on the Connecticut settlement of Wish-ton-Wish by the colonial Mark Heathcote and his family, their attack by Indians, and the kidnapping of Heathcote's young granddaughter Ruth, who later marries an Indian, Conanchet, and assumes the name Narra-mattah. Years later, when the settlement is again under attack by warring Indians, Conanchet and Narra-mattah save the captured Heathcotes from execution, wehreupon Conanchet is captured and executed, his wife dies beside the body of her husband, and her mother dies soon afterward, hence the "wept of Wish-ton-Wish." The influence of Rome's classical past is evident in Mozier's neo-classical treatment of the gentle contraposto stance and the graceful, if somewhat affected, gesture of the hand touching the chin. The figure's Indian "dress" is a modified classical tunic, with her sandals and shell ornaments on her head being the only indication of her assumed identity.

CHAUNCEY BRADLEY IVES, John Arnot, Sr.

JOSEPH MOZIER, The Wept of Wish-ton-Wish

ANTOINE-DENIS CHAUDET   French, 1763-1810

311 Amor Catching a Butterfly, 1802
Bronze 14 x 13$^{1}/_{2}$ x 8$^{3}/_{4}$ inches
Inscribed on base, top: Chaudet

PROVENANCE: Matthias H. Arnot, by 1879; by bequest to the Arnot Art Gallery, 1910.

LITERATURE: *Catalogue: Loan Exhibition* (Elmira, NY: n.p., 1879), p. 42, no. 1722; *Permanent Collection* (1973), p. 156.

Chaudet was born in Paris and, at age twenty-six, began his art training in paintings, studying under the neo-classical painters J. B. Stouf and Etienne Gois. In 1781, he won second prize in the Prix de Rome competition and three years later won first prize for his painting *Joseph Sold by His Brothers*. Chaudet later held a teaching position at the Ecole des Beaux-Arts where he edited a dictionary handbook to clarify and codify the language used in the school's courses. Establishing a reputation for both painting and sculpture, Chaudet regularly exhibited his neo-classical works in the Salons between 1798 and 1810. He received numerous state commissions, including one for an allegorical bas-relief placed in the courtyard of the Louvre, for a silver statue of *Paix* exhibited in the Tuileries, and for a sculpture of Cinncinatus for the French Senate. In 1805, he was named a menber of the Institut de France.

Amor Catching a Butterfly is a bronze replica of his marble original purchased by the state and now in the collection of the Louvre. Amor, the god of Love in Greek and Roman mythology, is depicted here as a winged, nude boy kneeling over the butterfly he has captured. The nascent Romantic movement in French art is evident in the artist's sensual treatment of the youth's firm flesh and the selection of a playful subject loosely based on an allegorical theme.

ANONYMOUS   French, 19th century

329 Mercury, n.d.
Bronze 25$^{1}/_{4}$ x 10$^{1}/_{4}$ x 10 inches
n.s.

PROVENANCE: Matthias H. Arnot, by 1879; by bequest to the Arnot Art Gallery, 1910.

LITERATURE: *Catalogue: Loan Exhibition* (Elmira, NY: n.p., 1879), p. 43, no. 1751; *Permanent Collection* (1973), p. 155 (as "Orpheus").

This work has been exhibited under the title of Orpheus, the legendary Thracian poet whose skill with the lyre had the ability to charm wild beasts, trees, and even rocks. Orpheus, however, is usually depicted with a laurel crown rather than wings, as in the Arnot figure. This work is closer to the iconography of Mercury, the messenger of the gods in Greek mythology. Usually depicted as a graceful male youth, Mercury's typical attributes are winged sandals and a winged hat to ensure his swift travel, although, in this rendition, wings protrude directly from his head. Mercury is also the inventor of the lyre and here he is shown holding the instrument on his hip, head down and right arm pulled back as if he had just plucked the strings. The static contraposto stance and the studied handling of anatomy suggest this work is by a competent if uninspired artist.

EGYPTIAN ARTIFACTS

Old Kingdom, First Intermediate Period, 2258-2052 BC
392 Ushabti
Black granite 4$^{1}/_{4}$ x 1$^{3}/_{16}$ x $^{15}/_{16}$ inches

Middle Kingdom, 2052-1570 BC
390 Head of Osiris
Quartz 4$^{1}/_{8}$ x 1$^{7}/_{8}$ x 2$^{5}/_{8}$ inches
394 Ushabti
Polychromed wood 7$^{1}/_{8}$ x 2$^{3}/_{16}$ x 1$^{3}/_{8}$ inches
395 Wall Fragment with Seated Man in Sunken Relief
Limestone 3$^{1}/_{4}$ x 2$^{3}/_{4}$ x 1$^{5}/_{8}$ inches
396 Wall Fragment with Hand in Bas-Relief
Limestone 3 x 1$^{1}/_{2}$ x 1$^{1}/_{4}$ inches
399 Cartouche of Ranoobkaoo
Faience 3$^{9}/_{16}$ x 1$^{1}/_{2}$ x $^{3}/_{8}$ inches

New Kingdom, 1185-950 BC
402 Ushabti
Faience 2$^{9}/_{16}$ x $^{3}/_{4}$ x $^{9}/_{16}$ inches
403 Ushabti
Faience 2$^{9}/_{16}$ x $^{3}/_{4}$ x $^{5}/_{8}$ inches

Late Period, 600-300 BC
391 Ushabti
Quartz 6$^{5}/_{16}$ x 2$^{3}/_{8}$ x 1$^{3}/_{4}$ inches
393 Ushabti
Faience 7$^{1}/_{16}$ x 1$^{7}/_{8}$ x 1$^{3}/_{8}$ inches
400 Vessel
Granite 1$^{1}/_{4}$ x 1$^{1}/_{4}$ x 1$^{1}/_{4}$ inches
401 Ushabti
Faience 4 x $^{1}/_{4}$ x $^{15}/_{16}$ inches

GREEK ARTIFACTS
848 Oinoche
Ceramic 5$^{15}/_{16}$ x 3$^{1}/_{2}$ x 3$^{3}/_{4}$ inches
849 Lekythos
Ceramic 8$^{1}/_{2}$ x 3$^{1}/_{4}$ x 3$^{1}/_{4}$ inches

ANTOINE-DENIS CHAUDET, Amor Catching a Butterfly

EGYPTIAN, quartz Ushabti

ANONYMOUS, Mercury

INDEX OF ARTISTS

ARTIST *PAGE NO.*

Bargue, Charles	78-79	Lorme, Anthonie de	*15*, 44-45
Barye, Antoine Louis	118-119	Lorrain, Claude	*9*, 38-39
Benjamin-Constant, Jean-Joseph	*23*, 86-87	Mancadan, Jacobus Sibrandi	48-49
Beyle, Pierre Marie	82-83	Marcke, Emile van	66-67
Bonheur, Auguste	80-81	Mazzolini, Guiseppe	116-117
Boughton, George Henry	110-111	Meissonier, Jean-Louis-Ernest	*20-21*, 70-71
Breton, Jules-Adolphe	*6*, 72-73	Merle, Hugues	88-89
Brueghel, Jan, the Elder	*11-12*, 50-53	Mérode, Carl von (Karl Freiherr von Mérode)	96-97
Chaudet, Antoine-Denis	124-125	Meyer, Johann Georg (Meyer von Bremen)	94-95
Champaigne, Jean-Baptiste de	*10*, 40-41	Millet, Jean-François	*16*, 68-69
Courbet, Gustave	*17*, 82-83	Mozier, Joseph	122-123
Cyphas, O.T.	116-117	Murillo, School of	56-57
Daubigny, Charles-François	*18*, 60-61	Nicol, Erskine	112-113
Denière, Guillaume	120-121	Rasinelli, Roberto	102-103
Diaz de la Peña, Narcisse Virgile	*19*, 62-63	Rico y Ortega, Martin	106-107
Dyck, Anthony van	58-59	Rottenhammer, Johann	*12*, 52-55
Eggert, Sigmund	100-101	Rousseau, Pierre Etienne Théodore	60-61
Fabri, A. E.	104-105	Rubens, Peter Paul	58-59
Falero, Luis Riccardo	104-105	Saintin, Jules-Emile	*24*, 84-85
Gérôme, Jean-Léon	*3*, 74-75	Sanchez-Perrier, Emilio	*4*, 104-105
Girard, Marie-François-Firmin	86-87	Schreyer, Adolphe	92-93
Glover, John	108-109	Steenwyck, Hendrik van, the Elder	46-47
Gros, Lucien-Alphonse	68-69	Street, Robert	116-117
Hiddeman, Friedrich Peter	94-95	Teniers, David, the Younger	*13*, 54-55
Hildebrandt, Ferdinand Theodor	92-93	Tetar van Elven, Pierre Henri	112-113
Hirt, Heinrich	100-101	Troyon, Constant	64-65
Hobbema, Meindert	58-59	Velde, Willem van de, (the Younger)	*14*, 42-43
Ives, Chauncey Bradley Ives	122-123	Verboeckhoven, Eugène Joseph	114-115
Jacque, Charles-Emile	62-63	Vibert, Jehan-Georges	*22*, 88-89
Kaemmerer, Frederick Hendrik	76-77	Vitringa, Wegerus	58-59
Knaus, Ludwig	*25*, 90-91	Weber, Paul	96-97
Leloir, Maurice	84-85	Wildens, Jan	58-59
Loefftz, Ludwig	98-99	Zuccoli, Luigi	102-103

Printed by Flower City Printing, Inc., Rochester,
on Productolith dull (Consolidated).
Set in Plantin Condensed by Typographics, Jacksonville.
Photography by Lesli Van Zandbergen.
Concept, design, and production by Jill Grossvogel,
Martin + Grossvogel Design, Ithaca.